THE FOREIGN LEADER PROGRAM

The Foreign Leader Program

OPERATIONS IN THE UNITED STATES

BY ROBERT E. ELDER
A Study Made at the Request of the Department of State

GREENWOOD PRESS, PUBLISHERS
WESTPORT, CONNECTICUT

Library of Congress Cataloging in Publication Data

Elder, Robert Ellsworth, 1915-
 The foreign leader program.

 "A Study made at the request of the Department of State [under an agreement with the Bureau of Educational and Cultural Affairs]"
 Reprint of the ed. published by the Brookings Institution, Washington, D. C.
 1. Exchange of persons programs, American. 2. Visitors, Foreign--United States. I. United States. Bureau of Educational and Cultural Affairs. II. Title.
 [E744.5.E45 1974]   353.008'92   74-11986
 ISBN 0-8371-7706-5

© *1961 by The Brookings Institution*

Originally published in 1961 by The Brookings Institution, Washington

Reprinted with the permission of The Brookings Institution

Reprinted in 1974 by Greenwood Press,
a division of Williamhouse-Regency Inc.

Library of Congress Catalog Card Number 74-11986

ISBN 0-8371-7706-5

Printed in the United States of America

THE BROOKINGS INSTITUTION is an independent organization devoted to nonpartisan research, education, and publication in economics, government, foreign policy, and the social sciences generally. Its principal purposes are to aid in the development of sound public policies and to promote public understanding of issues of national importance.

The Institution was founded December 8, 1927, to merge the activities of the Institute for Government Research, founded in 1916, the Institute of Economics, founded in 1922, and the Robert Brookings Graduate School of Economics and Government, founded in 1924.

The general administration of the Institution is the responsibility of a self-perpetuating Board of Trustees. In addition to this general responsibility, the By-Laws provide that, "It is the function of the Trustees to make possible the conduct of scientific research and publication, under the most favorable conditions, and to safeguard the independence of the research staff in the pursuit of their studies and in the publication of the results of such studies. It is not a part of their function to determine, control, or influence the conduct of particular investigations or the conclusions reached." The immediate direction of the policies, program, and staff of the Institution is vested in the President, who is assisted by an advisory council chosen from the professional staff of the Institution.

In publishing a study, the Institution presents it as a competent treatment of a subject worthy of public consideration. The interpretations and conclusions in such publications are those of the author or authors and do not necessarily reflect the views of other members of the Brookings staff or of the administrative officers of the Institution.

BOARD OF TRUSTEES

MOREHEAD PATTERSON, *Chairman*
ROBERT BROOKINGS SMITH, *Vice Chairman*
WILLIAM R. BIGGS, *Chairman, Executive Committee*

Arthur Stanton Adams
Dillon Anderson
Elliott V. Bell
Robert D. Calkins
Leonard Carmichael
Thomas H. Carroll
Edward W. Carter
Colgate W. Darden, Jr.
Marion B. Folsom
William C. Foster
Huntington Gilchrist

Huntington Harris
John E. Lockwood
Sydney Stein, Jr.
Gilbert F. White
Donald B. Woodward

Honorary Trustees

Daniel W. Bell
Mrs. Robert S. Brookings
John Lee Pratt

Foreword

THIS STUDY WAS PREPARED FOR the United States Department of State under an agreement with the Bureau of Educational and Cultural Affairs. In accepting the invitation of the Department to undertake the study, The Brookings Institution agreed to describe, analyze, and appraise the Foreign Leader Program, particularly to assess its present effectiveness and to suggest possibilities for improvement, both immediate and long-term.

It is hoped that the report will help not only to strengthen the administration of the program but to inform American citizens about a significant foreign policy program in which they have an opportunity to participate directly and usefully. Members of the Congress may gain greater knowledge of the program, of its possibilities and limitations, its problems and needs. Future foreign participants may obtain a better understanding of how to prepare for their tour of the United States, what to expect, and how to make the most of the opportunity. Other governments may comprehend the program more adequately.

The study is an attempt, with a limited budget, to identify the major problem areas and to suggest feasible improvements. Its field of interest is extensive; its recommendations, tentative rather than definitive. Use was made of work already done and of the experience and knowledge of those both inside and outside the Government who are intimately acquainted with the program. It is hoped that the information compiled, the methods used, and the experience gained may prove useful in the appraisal of other international exchange programs.

Approximately 120 interviews, ranging in duration from half an hour to three hours, were conducted by the author within a seven-week period from June 13 to July 29, 1960. Initially, broad problems were identified in nine interviews with leading individuals responsible for the conduct of the program in Washington. Additional interviews were conducted in the Bureau of Educational and Cultural Affairs, in several regional bureaus, and in the United States Information Agency, as well as with representatives of the American Council on Education's Committee on Leaders and Specialists, the Governmental Affairs Institute, the Department of Labor's Office of International Labor Affairs, and the Washington International Center.

Finally, interviews were conducted with personnel programming grantees in Philadelphia, New York, Boston, Cleveland, Chicago, Minneapolis, Bloomington (Indiana), Ashland and Bloomington (Illinois), and New Orleans. These cities were selected because they were believed to be representative of the wide variety of local communities dealing with grantees. Questionnaires were sent to the four Department of State reception centers which were not visited personally and to ten other local sponsors. These inquiries brought responses from Honolulu, San Francisco, Los Angeles, Seattle, Cedar Rapids, Buffalo, Albany, Pittsburgh, and Miami. Thus, by interview and questionnaire, responses were obtained from sixteen of the thirty-three communities most often used in the Foreign Leader Program and from four smaller communities used more sparingly (the latter played host to twenty-two, fourteen, seven, and one grantees respectively during fiscal year 1959). The cooperation of all those who contributed information is gratefully acknowledged.

The interviews were conducted and the basic draft of the study prepared by Robert E. Elder, Professor of Political Science, Colgate University, and director of the Washington study group, serving as a member of The Brookings Institution senior staff. Guidance, with review and suggestions, was provided throughout the period of research and writing by H. Field Haviland, Jr., Director of Foreign Policy Studies for The Brookings Institution, in consultation with Franklin P. Kilpatrick and Luther H. Evans of the Institution's senior staff.

In the preparation of the report, the author and members of The Brookings Institution staff associated with the study have had the benefit of consultation with an advisory committee consisting of Arthur Stanton Adams, President, American Council on Education;

René d'Harnoncourt, Director, Museum of Modern Art; Robert Estabrook, Editor of the editorial page, *The Washington Post;* Eric Larabee, Editor, *American Heritage;* Walter H. C. Laves, Chairman of the Department of Political Science, Indiana University; James L. Morrill, Consultant, The Ford Foundation; Lucian Pye, Professor of Political Science, Massachusetts Institute of Technology; and Frank Snowden, Dean, Howard University. The Institution is indebted to this group for many helpful suggestions.

The Institution presents the report as a competent treatment of a subject worthy of public consideration. Interpretations, however, are those of the author, and do not necessarily reflect the views of other members of the Brookings staff, its administrative officers, or its Board of Trustees.

ROBERT D. CALKINS
President

July 1961

Contents

FOREWORD vii

1. THE NATURE AND OBJECTIVES OF THE PROGRAM 1
   Relative Size and Trends 1
   Similarities and Differences in Exchange Programs 3
   A Typical Program 5
   Evolution of Exchange Programs 9
   Program Objectives 11
   One Hierarchy of Values? 12

2. OVERSEAS AND ARRIVAL PROCEDURES 15
   Standards of Selection 16
   The Process of Nomination and Selection 18
   Notification and Orientation 20
   Reception at Port of Entry 22
   Reception in Washington 26

3. NATION-WIDE PROGRAMMING 29
   The Program Areas of the Three Contract Agencies 30
   Programming the Foreign Leader 31
   Future Role of the Contract Agencies 34
   Improving Contract Agency Programming 36
   Per Diem Allowances 43
   Group Programs 44

4. ORIENTATION AND CROSS-CULTURAL COMMUNICATION 47
   The Washington International Center 48
   Improving the Orientation Process 51
   Escort-Interpreters 54
   Questions and Recommendations 56

5. COMMUNITY PARTICIPATION 62
   Programming Problems 64
   Alternate Emphases in Organization of Local Sponsors ... 72
   General Conclusions 78

6. TERMINAL PROCEDURES 80
   Terminal Seminars 81
   Evaluation before Departure 83
   Continuing Contacts Overseas 86

7. DEPARTMENTAL ADMINISTRATIVE PROBLEMS 89
   Operations: The Division and Branch Levels 90
   Planning and Evaluation 92
   Staffing the Program 95
   Budget and Fiscal Problems 96

8. CONCLUSIONS AND RECOMMENDATIONS 101
   1. The Nature and Objectives of the Program 101
   2. Overseas and Arrival Procedures 102
   3. Nation-wide Programming 103
   4. Orientation and Cross-cultural Communication 105
   5. Community Participation 107
   6. Terminal Procedures 108
   7. Departmental Administrative Problems 110

APPENDIXES

   A. Number of Completed Leader Visits, Fiscal Years 1956-1960 113
   B. Program Costs of Leader Exchanges: Obligations, Fiscal Years 1956-1960 114
   C. Bureau of Educational and Cultural Affairs, Department of State 115

1

The Nature and Objectives of the Program

THE FOREIGN LEADER PROGRAM of the Department of State is one of several efforts undertaken by the government of the United States to encourage the extensive and intensive exchange of ideas among peoples and nations. Each year it arranges study tours in the United States for nine hundred or more nationals of other countries who have been selected for their leadership roles. It has been a significant pioneering experiment in improving relations with key people from other lands as a step toward establishing stronger foundations for international cooperation. The present study is primarily an appraisal of the operation of the program in the United States.

RELATIVE SIZE AND TRENDS

Exchange of persons is a two-way street. In recent years, under Department of State and International Cooperation Administration programs, some 20,000 to 22,500 foreign nationals and American citizens annually have taken part in international exchange activities. Approximately 70 to 75 per cent of the participants are foreign nationals who come to the United States for periods of study and observation; the remainder are Americans sent abroad.

Department of State programs, administered chiefly by the Bureau of Educational and Cultural Affairs, have involved between

6,000 and 7,000 individuals each year since 1957. In addition, the bureau provides assistance in one way or another to about the same number of individuals participating in exchange programs conducted under the auspices of private organizations, either domestic or foreign. While the bureau's own programs are weighted more than two to one toward bringing foreign nationals to the United States, the ratio is reversed in the private programs.

The Foreign Leader Program was inaugurated by the Department of State in 1947. From fiscal year 1951, when the post-World War II reorientation of German leaders was at its peak, to fiscal year 1960, the number of persons brought to the United States annually under the Foreign Leader Program declined steadily from approximately 1,900 to 714. Most of these foreign leaders traveled individually about the United States, but there has been a recent trend toward more group planning. Partly as a result of such group projects, the downward trend was reversed in fiscal year 1961 when well over 900 foreign leaders were brought to the United States. The figure will be higher in fiscal year 1962, although the Department continues to advocate a policy of quality rather than quantity.

The impact of world-wide exchanges of persons, which have been conducted for more than fourteen years, is becoming increasingly visible as foreign nationals trained in America under both short- and long-range programs move into positions of responsibility. But the recent upward trend in the Foreign Leader Program can be attributed to no simple cause. Among the contributing factors have been the dramatization of the potentialities of all forms of cross-cultural exchange by initiation of exchange programs with the Soviet Union, the renewed attention to Latin America in the wake of the Vice President's 1958 visit to that area, the rapid emergence of independent African states, the deterioration of Soviet-American relations after the collapse of the summit talks in the spring of 1960, and the favorable attitude of the Kennedy administration toward exchange, symbolized by elevating the head of the Bureau of Educational and Cultural Affairs to Assistant Secretary rank.

SIMILARITIES AND DIFFERENCES IN EXCHANGE PROGRAMS

For the sake of clarity, there is need to distinguish the Foreign Leader Program from other governmental exchange programs. The task is not easy. Although the Leader Program has distinctive characteristics, it has elements in common with other programs. The differences are matters of definition and emphasis in purposes, procedures, and participants.

Students who come here or go abroad on study grants under Department of State auspices are carefully selected and are among those from whom community, state, and national leaders are likely to develop over the years. Teachers and professors who are exchanged to teach or engage in research have a somewhat more immediate impact upon opinion through their teaching or writing, as well as through participation in civic affairs. Businessmen, labor technicians, agricultural specialists and others who are brought to the United States by the International Cooperation Administration may have considerable influence upon public opinion in their homelands, as do most of the specialists brought to America by the Department of State.

The special emphasis of the Foreign Leader Program was stated in a memorandum of December 6, 1960, included in the briefing book assembled by the Department of State for incoming Secretary Dean Rusk.

> The Foreign Leader Program is intended to develop in other countries an informed nucleus of influential persons who, as a result of their observations and experiences in this country, can be expected to present to their own people an accurate and understanding interpretation of the United States and its people.

Participants are picked by the United States Government and are brought to this country for relatively short visits, averaging about 45 days although sometimes running to 60 or 90 days. As pointed out by one of the Department's exchange program veterans, writing in

Adult Education (Autumn 1956), the foreign visitors brought under the Leader Program

> are the governors of states, the rectors of universities, the members of national or state legislatures or city or county legislative bodies, the leading lights in the creative arts, writing, music, drama, and so forth. [They may be labor leaders or museum directors; men in high political office or those likely to assume positions of greater responsibility.] In short, they are the sort of people anyone would select if he were looking about the United States for leaders and persons of genuine influence whose words will always not only be heard, but heeded.

The Foreign Specialists Program, the most closely related of all other governmental exchange programs, and administered by the same division of the Department of State, has the same general objectives as those stated above for the Foreign Leader Program "but provides in addition an opportunity for practical experience or training in the visitor's field of endeavor." Participants are selected in the same manner as for the Leader Program. They tend to be somewhat younger, stay in the United States on the average for a longer period of time, and receive less per diem. They are more interested in acquiring knowledge in a specific field than are most leaders. In this respect, the Foreign Specialists Program is similar to some International Cooperation Administration exchange programs.

The purpose of the technical cooperation programs as stated in the Mutual Security Act is, in part, "to aid the efforts of the peoples of economically underdeveloped areas to develop their resources and improve their working and living conditions by encouraging the exchange of technical knowledge and skills. . . ." International Cooperation Administration (ICA) exchange programs are based on bilateral project agreements with foreign countries, and selection of the participants is a joint process between the United States and foreign governments. Many of these exchanges are conducted on a group basis in contrast to the individual nature of most Foreign Leader or Foreign Specialists Program exchanges. But the latter programs are increasing their emphasis upon group programming. Although ICA programs are not designed specifically to impart knowledge of the United States that will enable the exchangees "to present to their own people an accurate and understanding interpretation of the United States and its people," this is often a side effect of their visits. As ICA moves into the field of individual exchanges for longer periods of time in American educational institutions, it approaches the kinds of experiences hitherto found mostly in educational exchanges of the Department of State under the Fulbright and Smith-Mundt Acts.

The Board of Foreign Scholarships, in its report of February 27, 1961, to the President, speaks of the educational exchange programs of the Department of State as "strictly educational in character." Grants are awarded for "graduate study, elementary and secondary school teaching and teacher training, university lecturing, advanced research and comparable educational activities." Participants are often in the United States for periods of a year and are selected through "extensive cooperation between American and foreign administrators of the program." Grantees "must prepare serious projects for their work under the grants." Like participants in the Foreign Leader Program, however, they "must also demonstrate an ability . . . to communicate to their fellow citizens the results of their experience."

Some foreign nationals might qualify for grants from either the International Cooperation Administration or the Department of State, for teaching, lecturing, or research, as specialists or leaders. As a matter of fact, there is some shopping around by foreign nationals to determine which grants, among the variety available, best suit their individual needs. There is also some cooperation among American agencies overseas in finding the program for which a foreign national can qualify. If the exchange programs are not mutually exclusive or so refined that they serve only one purpose, neither are they so broad that they serve identical purposes. There still are capable foreign nationals and American citizens who qualify for participation under only one category.

A TYPICAL PROGRAM

Although the programs of no two persons under the Foreign Leader Program are likely to be exactly the same, many programs follow patterns that are somewhat similar in character. A composite model can, therefore, provide a useful overview of the Foreign Leader Program.

A typical leader, whether he be European, Asian, African, or Latin American, is probably unofficially aware that his name has been placed in nomination for a grant long before an Embassy representative, perhaps the Ambassador, notifies him of his final selection. From others who have previously had such grants or from informal discussions with Embassy officials, he may have gained some idea of what he will do during his 60-day study tour of the United States. On the other hand, he may know nothing of the program prior to notification of his selection.

Before the grantee leaves for the United States, the Department of State normally has received biographic information from the overseas post, along with a statement of what the grantee wants to do in the United States, what he feels is the purpose of his trip, and what the cultural affairs officer at the Embassy hopes the grantee will gain from the visit.

Some discussion and orientation regarding the program takes place between an Embassy representative and the foreign leader before the grantee flies to the United States, perhaps arriving in New York City on a weekend. There he may simply transfer from one plane to another and continue on to Washington or he may stop for a day or so before proceeding farther. At the New York airport, he is met and assisted by one of three full-time employees assigned to airport duty by the Department of State's New York reception center.

In Washington, he is welcomed at the airport by a representative of the Department of State. On the first working day in Washington, he will meet with an area officer of the Leaders Branch, Bureau of Educational and Cultural Affairs, for an initial interview. He will then be introduced to a program officer in one of the three agencies programming foreign leaders under contract with the Department of State. These agencies are: the American Council on Education's Committee on Leaders and Specialists, the Governmental Affairs Institute, and the Office of International Labor Affairs of the Department of Labor.

A visitor will remain in Washington from a week to ten days. During this time he may do some sightseeing, perhaps straying beyond Mount Vernon to Williamsburg, consult with professional colleagues in the city or nearby areas, talk with governmental officials interested in his field, possibly attend a two-day Conference on American Life at the Washington International Center, and meet on several occasions with his program officer to help plan his study tour. He can take an active role in designing his own program since visitors are "invited to come to this country at their own convenience to follow their own interest."

During the Washington portion of the visit, the program officer is busily engaged in piecing together a workable program—arranging transportation and schedules as well as purchasing air, rail, or bus tickets—and is beginning to notify sponsors in local communities of the visitor's interests and dates of arrival and departure.

If the visitor is staying the full 60 days—many of them are here for only half this time or less—he is likely to take the "grand tour." Program sponsors in cities on this circuit take care of well over 150 leader visitors each year, plus many foreign nationals coming under other programs. Several sponsors handle 450 to 800 leaders annually. These cities are of sufficient size and have a broad enough range of program opportunities to attract visitors with interests in almost any field.

In each city, the grantee is likely to consult with professional colleagues, visit local tourist attractions, attend cultural and civic events, and enjoy some form of hospitality with an American family, whether it be a picnic, a dinner, an evening watching television, or informal conversation. In addition to stops in these larger cities, he will visit at least one smaller community, of 50,000 population or less, perhaps escaping the typical moderately priced hotel for a visit in an American home for several days.

The program sponsors in these cities will be a Department of State reception center, the local office of the Institute for International Education, which programs grantees on contract for the Department, or private organizations such as a university, a Council on World Affairs, a chamber of commerce, or an interested family in a small town such as Ashland, Illinois, population 1,100.

After saying good-by to his program officer in Washington, the grantee, accompanied by an escort-interpreter if his knowledge of

English is insufficient for him to fend for himself, flies to New York City for a four-day stop; to Boston for two days; to Buffalo for a two-day visit and a side visit to Niagara Falls; onward to Detroit for several days, and thence to Chicago for a week's stopover.

He may then be routed to a small town for a few days, perhaps Ashland or Bloomington, Illinois, both of which are in Lincoln country, each in its own way a typical Midwestern community. Catching a plane at Springfield, Illinois, the visitor flies to Denver, arriving there before his local hosts who took him to the airport are back in Ashland or Bloomington.

After a short stay in Denver, he may take a side visit to a scenic small Colorado community before flying on to San Francisco, California. Four days there will be followed by a visit to sprawling Los Angeles, with Hollywood as a prime attraction. Foreign visitors usually look forward to New Orleans, which has more of an Old World atmosphere than most American cities, but it is not unusual for them to stop in Arizona for a look at the Grand Canyon. Knoxville, Tennessee, which gained world-wide fame because of the Tennessee Valley Authority, is likely to be the last stop before the visitor returns to Washington for final interviews with his program officer in the contracting agency and his area officer in the Leaders Branch of the Department of State. Possibly he will participate with several other grantees in a three-day terminal seminar on "the American scene." He may be interviewed by the Voice of America for a radio program to be beamed to his home country provided he is willing.

After this itinerary and its assorted experiences usually crammed into a 60-day period or less, the grantee flies to New York City for a final stopover of several days for rest and recreation—including the purchase of presents for members of his family—before boarding his plane for the return to his native land. At this point the direct responsibility of the Department's Leaders Branch ends, and the American Embassy in the grantee's homeland takes over and follows through in either a formal or informal manner to maintain a relationship with the grantee and to evaluate the results of the visit.

The cost to the United States is likely to have been between $3,500 and $7,000, averaging about $4,800. This money was expended for a per diem allowance to the grantee of $20 to $25, for travel expenses in the United States up to $550, for a $50 allowance for the purchase of books by the grantee, perhaps for provision of an interpreter-escort, for administrative expenses of the Department of State and the contracting agencies who assisted with his program, and for the international transportation of the visitor.

In addition to the sum officially expended, private individuals across America provide food and lodging, entertainment and sightseeing, with costs which are not calculated by the Department of State and which cannot be accurately estimated. The organizations responsible for playing host in most of the cities carry some burden of administrative cost from funds largely raised in annual drives. The dentist and his wife who have entertained seven grantees as home visitors over the past two years in Ashland, Illinois, bear this cost out of their own pockets. In passing, it may be noted that the recent emphasis on programming grantees as groups rather than as individuals was done partly to reduce the workload of cooperating personnel and to cut costs.

This recitation of the effort involved in programming a single foreign leader by such diverse personnel—Embassy representatives overseas, Department of State personnel, the agencies, the local sponsors, and many private individuals—raises the question of what the Foreign Leader Program's purposes and objectives have been and should be.

EVOLUTION OF EXCHANGE PROGRAMS

The concept of exchanging persons and ideas on both an informal and formal, private and public, basis is far from new. Exploration, trade, and religion early served as catalysts to bring peoples together. Diplomatic and consular representation followed in the wake of such activities. Private travel, including permanent migration, broadened cross-cultural contacts. Even the movement of troops during time of war served to increase knowledge of persons and cultures lying beyond national frontiers. The growth of business, professional, and other private associations organized internationally provided added impetus to the exchange of persons and ideas. The role of the United States Government in such matters, except in official diplomatic and consular activities, was at best intermittent before 1936.

The shadow of war hung heavy over the Inter-American Conference for the Maintenance of Peace at Buenos Aires in 1936 when the United States proposed the "Facilitation by Government Action of the Exchange of Students and Teachers." The exploitation of education as an instrument of national policy by Hitler and Mussolini and the threat of Nazi penetration in Latin America had quickened the pace of the Good Neighbor policy. A Convention for the Promotion of Inter-American Cultural Relations was adopted by the conference and ratified by the U.S. Senate in 1938. Implementing legislation, in the form of Public Laws 63 and 355, 75th Congress, was passed in 1939. No additional legislation regarding cultural relations was enacted until 1946.

The Second World War brought reluctant recognition by the American people of the need for greater peacetime participation in world affairs. In the field of cultural relations, the so-called Fulbright Act of 1946, Public Law 584, 79th Congress, authorized the use of foreign currencies for educational exchange purposes. The United States Information and Educational Exchange Act of 1948, Public Law 402, 80th Congress, known as the Smith-Mundt Act, authorized broad reciprocal educational exchange programs between the United States and other countries and the annual appropriation of funds for such purposes. These two acts remain the foundation of the Department of State's cultural relations programs today.

If the threat of Nazi penetration sparked a Latin American emphasis in the Department of State's cultural exchange programs after 1938, it was fear of a possible resurgence of nazism in Germany and of Communist penetration of postwar Europe which triggered a new European emphasis as cold-war tensions heightened in the period after 1948.

As the Marshall Plan and the North Atlantic Treaty Organization helped achieve some degree of stability in Europe, tensions of international conflict were extended beyond the continent to less developed areas where political, economic, and social conditions were more precarious. The spotlight turned toward the Far East, South Asia, and the Middle East. The cultural exchange programs of the Department of State adjusted to this emphasis. More recently, growing unrest in Latin America and the emergence of the new African nations have forced another shift of general American foreign policy and exchange programs toward these areas.

Through the years, American governmental exchange programs have progressed from inaction to counteraction. After an early period of almost casual development, American governmental cultural exchange programs were sponsored as responses to specific challenges to national security. Even though they appeared more positive than other aspects of national policy, their explicit and implicit objectives, organization, and procedures were colored by the challenges they were established to meet. Today, there is a question of whether the American response continues to be oriented primarily "against" threats to its national security posed by foreign governments with differing ideologies—a reaction pattern first developed over two decades ago in response to Nazi pressures in Latin America. Or are American exchange programs beginning to emphasize a more positive response, stressing the need for a freer and more intensive merging of thought and action?

PROGRAM OBJECTIVES

The relatively simple statement of the basic purpose of the Foreign Leader Program incorporated in the briefing book for incoming Secretary Rusk in December 1960 may become a beacon for those who welcome a more positive emphasis in American foreign policy:

> The Foreign Leader Program is intended to develop in other countries an informed nucleus of influential persons who, as a result of their observations and experiences in this country, can be expected to present to their own people an accurate and understanding interpretation of the United States and its people.

The mere formulation of such a statement does not, of course, guarantee its implementation. As a matter of fact, the United States Information and Educational Exchange Act of 1948 was enacted "to promote a better understanding of the United States in other countries and to increase mutual understanding between the people of the United States and the people of other countries." Because this statement applied to all Department of State exchange of persons programs, it was the broadest and most fundamental objective of the Foreign Leader Program.

But the Exchange Act's positive note was somewhat limited in practice during the first thirteen years. Supplemental statements, which spelled out more detailed objectives, were issued from time to time. On occasion, they seemed out of step with the earlier and more general statement of purpose, or at least they allowed a variety of conflicting interpretations. These more specific statements sometimes appeared to be adapted to various types of audiences. Problems of intercommunication and differences in motivation among program operators, loosely directed from Washington and scattered not only across the United States but around the world, may also have contributed to the difficulty of achieving the broad purposes of the Exchange Act.

The fact that leaders were coming to America for "consultation with colleagues" was stressed in the invitations issued overseas by American Embassy representatives. Readers of American periodicals were apprised that the leaders were brought to get "the full and fair picture of the contemporary American scene." Members of the House Appropriations Committee were told that the program would contribute to meeting emergency "political developments." All three of these emphases were to be accomplished while granting "freedom of action" to the leaders during their visits. Although statements such as the four recounted here are not necessarily in conflict, they have contributed to some confusion among program operators. Whatever the cause of differences among the various statements of purpose, the variations leave room for substantial differences in interpretation. The interviews underlying this study revealed widely varying interpretations by program officers in Washington, contractors, volunteers, the foreign leaders themselves, and their escort-interpreters.

ONE HIERARCHY OF VALUES?

Against this background, it is useful to take a closer look at the Foreign Leader Program's present objectives. If the desire to formulate a hierarchy of values to govern the programming of all foreign leaders is unrealistic, there is a need to clarify the relationship among competing values so that a well-defined sense of direction can be projected from the Department of State to correct whatever confusion may exist in the minds of program operators in the field. At the same time, there is a justifiable desire for some degree of flexibility in programming so that leaders with diverse backgrounds and personalities may be handled differently. Some leaders need to be brought to the United States for special purposes which fall within the general objectives of both the memorandum in the briefing book prepared for Secretary Rusk and the Exchange Act of 1948 but which do not allow enough time for a broader look at America.

It is recommended, therefore, that one major cluster of values be projected as the guide for programming what may be called typical leaders. Other values should be projected on a somewhat more individual basis for leaders who come to achieve more specific knowledge or to fulfill special purposes consistent with but narrower than the general objectives of the program.

It is suggested that typical leaders have freedom of action to do what they wish so long as it contributes to the acquisition of "the full and fair picture of the contemporary American scene" in order that they will be in a position after the visit "to present to their own people an accurate and understanding interpretation of the United States and its people." Consultation with colleagues should be only a means to this end. Within limits, conversations with counterparts will help a visitor to obtain a picture of the American scene, but talking only with counterparts may prevent a "full and fair" or well-rounded picture.

To suggest that a particular value system be projected to operators in the field to govern the programming of most leaders is not to imply that the program must become inflexible. Coupled with the adoption of a general value system for typical leader programs should be a recognition that leaders brought for special purposes should be given special handling. A labor leader whose labor union has been infiltrated by Communists can be brought to America under the Leader Program for consulation with union leaders who have dealt successfully with this problem. An educational leader who is about to make a revision of the curriculum of the elementary schools in his country can be brought to America to talk with educational leaders here. But the controlling value system to be furthered during such visits should provide general guidance for those associated with programming the visitor.

There are, unfortunately, other leaders with whom very little can be accomplished by any educational program—men who do not want to learn the realities of American or international life, who prefer to play upon the half-truths and lack of knowledge which enslave great portions of the human race, or whose interests are personal gratification rather than the good of their peoples. In some instances, it may be that American interests would be better served if their desires were satisfied elsewhere without having them set foot in the United States. Fortunately, this type of individual is confined to a reasonably small proportion of the leaders now coming to America under the Foreign Leader Program.

2

Overseas and Arrival Procedures

THE TYPES OF LEADERS SELECTED for participation in the Foreign Leader Program and the orientation they receive determine in large measure the kinds of substantive experiences and operational procedures which are likely to be most effective in achieving the program's objectives.

There is no open competition for foreign leader grants. On the basis of criteria laid down by the Bureau of Educational and Cultural Affairs, candidates are nominated by overseas posts and either approved or rejected by the bureau after consultation with the appropriate regional bureau of the Department of State. Candidates are notified of their selection by the local American Embassy and, if they accept the invitation, they are then given some orientation concerning the nature of the grant as well as general information about the United States.

When a leader accepts an invitation, the Bureau of Educational and Cultural Affairs is informed of the tentative date when he will begin travel under his grant. Tickets for roundtrip international travel are procured by the Embassy when the visitor's plans are definite. Before he leaves for the United States, the post issues a travel allowance of $70, which is intended to cover his miscellaneous expenses in traveling both from and to his own country, and notifies the bureau of the expected time and date of arrival.

STANDARDS OF SELECTION

The criteria for selection, formally stated in the International Educational Exchange Manual, declare that candidates for foreign leader grants must, in addition to being citizens of the country in which they are selected, (1) "enjoy good health, be of good moral character, and eligible for a United States visa;" (2) "have a working knowledge of the English language unless arrangements can be made to furnish them with interpreter services;" (3) "be leaders at the local, state or national levels" who do or are expected to exercise "significant influence over important organizations and institutions or substantial segments of public opinion;" and (4) "possess sufficient maturity, good judgment and fair-mindedness to ensure maximum benefits from their programs" and not have "personality characteristics" which would "substantially limit their receptiveness to new ideas" or "seriously impair their relationships with Americans."[1]

On the surface these criteria appear to be reasonable and clearly stated, but in practice they have been subjected to a variety of interpretations and all but ignored if the leader seemed likely to wield enough "significant influence," although sometimes even this criterion seems to have been overlooked. Problem cases—problems from the point of view of those programming leaders in the United States—are troublesome though infrequent. It may be assumed that a high proportion of such problems arise from the importance assigned to the "influence" factor as a criterion of selection—whether it be the individual's position or that of a close relative. Some problems may arise from an honest lack of knowledge about the individual being considered or from a failure to make a careful check of the facts concerning all criteria. Or it may be that cross-cultural experiences are more difficult with some cultures than with others.

The program as currently organized is able to function relatively smoothly if the criteria for selection are scrupulously observed. This study indicates that a very large proportion of grantee experiences—probably 80 to 90 per cent—are successful. If a more careful screen-

[1] The criteria for selection are undergoing revision for inclusion in a new manual (an informal publication for use inside the State Department).

ing is to be done, either the number of leaders will have to be curtailed or more effort will have to be devoted to the process of selection in the field. There is evidence that some improvement in overseas procedures is necessary.

Also important are such mundane considerations as the time of year when the leader will be available so that the program load in the United States can be more or less stable and foreign leaders may be given reasonable treatment at all times. Though embassies in small countries may find it more difficult to schedule their leader visitors evenly, the importance of spacing visits throughout the year—while meeting the needs of the foreign leaders—should be stressed. Alternate nominations and selections should be made in fields that can be programmed by the same contract agency as that indicated for the original nominee so that one does not find a musician being programmed by the Governmental Affairs Institute because the governmental leader who was originally selected could not come.

There is some question regarding the level of leadership that should be considered for nomination. Unfortunately, it is difficult to compare the level of journalists, for example, with the level of parliamentarians. Suffice it to say that men of real influence, who are highly visible in their own societies, are more likely to be productive exchange investments than those of less significance selected to fill quotas. While promising younger leaders should be considered, selection at this level must be judged by the most rigorous standards.

There is the danger, however, that visits by figures of high rank may disintegrate into a series of ceremonial events which fail to achieve the basic purposes of the program. Such notables may not be suited for inclusion in the program as it is now implemented and perhaps should be handled outside regular channels. It may be best to give preference to those in the middle range who are in the process of "arriving" or have only recently arrived and to make other provision for those few men of the highest rank.

The question of over-all balance in selection between developed and underdeveloped countries, between civilizations more like our own and those with quite different cultures, is a problem which cannot be settled by the foreign post. The emphasis will have to be adjusted to meet the changing circumstances of the times. In choosing among leaders who already agree generally with American views, who are wavering between East and West, or who are considered to have anti-Western attachments, the program has moved toward some degree of balance among the three categories and has provided itself with satisfactory procedures for assuring itself of a considerable range of views among the leaders.

The problem of whether to allow wives to accompany their husbands has been a persistent one. Not only does their presence add to the cost of the tour; often wives do not have the same interests as their husbands and must be programmed or entertained separately to keep them occupied while their husbands accomplish the purposes of the visit. On the other hand, when the Department's policy did not take them into account, they arrived sometimes separately on their own funds, turned up quite unexpectedly, and upset plans already made by local program officers. On balance, it does not appear that even all married leaders being scheduled individually in the United States should be accompanied by their wives, but in some circumstances it may be advisable. The selection of wives requires Embassy discretion. It should be a general rule, however, that wives should not be allowed to accompany leaders brought to the United States for group programs.

THE PROCESS OF NOMINATION AND SELECTION

Where the nomination process is well organized, names and information about the candidates will be collected and reviewed by United States Information Service officers and by Foreign Service officers in cities with consular or other government posts in cooperation with representatives of other foreign affairs agencies and with local representatives of various American enterprises. Some consultation with leading local citizens may be used as a cross-check.

Final decisions on nominations will be made in the Embassy, ideally drawing upon the "country team," which includes the cultural affairs officer. While the latter has administrative responsibility for the conduct of the exchange program, and should be the key figure in the selection process, a growing interest in the Foreign Leader Program as a tool of foreign policy may tend to take the actual selection of candidates out of his hands. He is a representative of the United States Information Agency and normally not a member of the Foreign Service. Because cultural affairs tend to be considered one step below political, economic, and military affairs in embassies abroad, the cultural affairs officer may suffer somewhat from lack of prestige. The committee on nominations is as likely to be chaired by the deputy chief of mission or the counselor for political affairs as by the cultural affairs officer. Some wonder if this situation has not led to an overemphasis in the selection of politically oriented grantees, including so-called parliamentary groups, in search of short-term political impact with little reference to more basic long-range gains.

No one in the Department, however, either in the Bureau of Educational and Cultural Affairs or in the geographic bureaus, is likely to overrule a nomination except for some administrative reason. While the power to overrule the field is present, the Department normally accepts what the post wants because it feels that "the post is in a better position to know the nominee."

Information submitted to the Department with the nomination includes the following: full name, place and date of birth, citizenship, home or permanent mailing address, academic training, present position, significant positions held in the past, membership in professional organizations, publications, foreign travel, knowledge of English, candidate's purposes and planned activities, and preferred dates of travel. Also forwarded are the post's objectives in nominating the candidate as well as supplementary information concerning the candidate's personality, political leanings, personal outlook, and attitude toward the United States.

On the whole, this procedure works reasonably well when the basic regulations are observed and all officials involved have sufficient time and interest to participate actively in the process. Sometimes embassy domination of selection or non-selection is embarrassing. Problems can arise when an ambassador invites a foreign leader on the spur of the moment without checking carefully into his background and the other circumstances relevant to the proposed visit. Problems may stem from excessive enthusiasm of a cultural affairs officer or other members of the country team in using the program as a crash solution to their problems, overlooking the criteria for selection or other limits of the program.

What cannot be done well should not be done at all. This is not to say that foreign leaders who do not meet the criteria of the program are to be ignored by Foreign Service officers in the field. But one need not invite everyone with whom he does business into his home. Foreign leaders may be courted, entertained, or dealt with overseas in a variety of ways, but all persons of significant influence do not have to be run through the Leader Program. Irreparable damage can be done to program resources in the United States through misuse of the enterprise.

NOTIFICATION AND ORIENTATION

Formal orientation of the leader can begin with notification of his selection or can be postponed until after acceptance of the invitation. The Embassy states the purpose of the nomination in the nominating letter. If the potential visitor has displayed some but not exceptional enthusiasm about the trip, it may seem desirable to stimulate acceptance. It is possible to emphasize that the visitor is to be the guest of the Department of State and that he will have complete freedom of action for consultation with colleagues in the United States. The problem with this approach is that it arouses expectations of "red-carpet" treatment which will not be, and cannot be, satisfied as the program presently operates. To make matters worse, this approach may encourage the man to feel that he can do anything he wants to do at the expense of the American taxpayer. In view of the number of visitors who have already come, certain of his colleagues in the United States—those he probably most wants to see —may be less than enthusiastic about welcoming him.

While the motive behind the attempt to give the feeling of complete freedom can be understood, this approach may be more likely to arouse suspicions than if the limits of the program are discussed frankly. The limits are not intended to prevent a fair look at America but to make it possible. Most foreign leaders know full well that one does not get something for nothing. What the United States wants from them is the fair, full look at America. When they hear about "complete freedom," they may suspect either deception or naïveté.

If the approach is flattering to the ego of the foreign leader, it makes it somewhat difficult for the cultural affairs officer to carry on any realistic orientation for the trip. Lack of such orientation puts the officials in the contract agency in a difficult position. They are almost forced to program a strong-willed visitor in a manner to meet his expectations of freedom, which may be close to license and which may make it almost impossible to accomplish the basic purposes of the Embassy. An equally strong-willed program officer may attempt to make suggestions and set limitations which may alienate the visitor.

No one wants American taxpayers to subsidize mere vacation trips. Visitors primarily interested in professional contacts might be better dealt with under the Foreign Specialists Program—if its per diem limitation were raised to a more satisfactory level—or given special handling within the Leader Program. Leaders who are primarily seeking prestige might, if they warrant the effort, be specially programmed and handled outside the normal Foreign Leader Program. Granted that almost every grantee will share some of these motivations, those who are accepted should have as their primary goal an honest desire to learn more about the over-all American scene. To achieve this goal in the time available, it will be necessary to provide suitable accommodations and some individual attentions which recognize the grantee's status, allow him some time for relaxation and reflection, and arrange for him to talk with some of his counterparts in the United States as a helpful bridge to successful cross-cultural relations.

Some have suggested that the invitation indicate that the typical visitor is to be the guest of the American people, instead of the Department of State, or that the grant is comparable to a short-term traveling fellowship instead of consultation with colleagues. The present phrasing should be carefully reconsidered. The Department transfers responsibility for the visitor so quickly to private agencies that this often comes as a surprise and something of a blow to the grantee. So long as the Department is not to handle the visitor's program in its entirety, it might be better if the wording of the original invitation were reframed to avoid this "let down" feeling.

It may be that a few leaders should be invited as guests of the Department of State—for example, when the visit is intended to be a substitute for a state visit. In these instances, the program must be of a special nature to match the implications of the invitation.

To the extent that the "traveling fellowship" idea is emphasized with the implied responsibility for a serious look at the American scene, the need for some orientation both before and after arriving in America would appear more justifiable. If the grantee fears indoctrination, the proof of the pudding would be in the eating. Properly handled, such sessions can indicate to the grantee that, while it is hoped that he will gain a broad understanding of the American scene, the United States does not expect slavish agreement.

The overseas post currently has the responsibility of "providing each leader, prior to departure, with appropriate informative material about the United States" and with "full clarification of the various aspects of the grant and such other information as the posts feel desirable in each individual case." Leaders are presented a "traveler's handbook" and a pamphlet describing "life in the United States." In the hustle of arranging their personal affairs in order to get off, many leaders are not particularly interested in even this limited amount of pre-departure orientation. What is done, therefore, should be more in the nature of creating a general attitude toward the experience than trying to cram substantive knowledge into minds that are not receptive. In some cases it may be possible to do more, but the cultural affairs officer may not be the individual best suited to conduct the orientation. Too much dependence on formal briefing materials must be avoided, the leaders expect individualized treatment.

The need for orientation to enable the visitor to get the most from his trip in the minimum amount of time should be emphasized. No trip is likely to be worth its cost if it is a kaleidoscopic jumble of unrelated bits and pieces. One can hardly expect the average foreign leader to gain even a minimum understanding of America in two months or less without some systematic preparation.

RECEPTION AT PORT OF ENTRY

A stranger in a foreign land, a leader grantee may be unsure of himself as he steps out of the plane amid the bustle of an international airport. Often tired and unshaven, his routine of life shaken, he may look and feel little like a leader of significant influence.

Normally, the visitor is met "in customs." Several other grantees may have come in the same plane, so the attention he gets may be shared. A major reception center, like that of New York or Honolulu, will greet 2,500 to 4,000 persons per year. This is a process that can become quite mechanical. Though it may appear to be a routine job, the ability to size up the visitor on sight and to give him the type of reception he needs requires skill and sensitivity. An excessively hearty greeting can be as abrasive as sandpaper. A gentle welcome may appear too casual.

Occasionally the grantee and the greeter miss connections. The visitor may arrive early or late. "No show" is common in the reports of the greeters. What can be a heart-warming reception at its best may turn into a chilling experience of standing in line alone through immigration and customs. As one person summed it up, commenting upon Public Health, Immigration and Naturalization, and Customs operations, "The inspection services are primarily possessed of a 'police' mentality. To these services, human beings are divided into 'Americans,' 'diplomats,' and 'foreigners'."

Reception of foreign visitors coming under Department of State or International Cooperation Administration auspices, plus regular diplomatic arrivals, is only one function of a Department of State reception center. Local residents of the six communities in which the reception centers are located call on center personnel regarding all types of problems related to foreign relations. The reception center programmers plan visits in the locality for the Foreign Leader and Foreign Specialist Programs, and also take care of voluntary visitors whose programs are organized by the Department of State. Several of the reception centers are used heavily as part of the grand tour of the United States undertaken by most leader grantees. New York and San Francisco receive half or more of the leaders on tour; New Orleans and Miami, a quarter or slightly less; Seattle and Honolulu, about 5 to 10 per cent.[2]

New Orleans is a two-officer center, with one secretary. The two Foreign Service officers make most of the international "meets"

---

[2] A seventh reception center was established in Washington subsequent to the making of this study. It has no programming responsibilities. Since it functions in Washington, area residents do not use it as a major source of information on Department of State affairs.

in New Orleans as part of their over-all duties in the reception center there. Occasionally they request an airline public relations representative to meet visitors for them when they are exceptionally busy programming leader or specialist grantees. The number of their meets in January 1960 was 87 (53 in one plane); for the ensuing months, February through June, the number of meets ran 10, 8, 45, 29, and 28. During the same six months, the two officers arranged programs for 15, 65, 53, 83, 71 and 92 visitors. These figures indicate the general workload which appears to be relatively heavy.

San Francisco is staffed by three persons of officer level, plus one lower-ranking civil servant who does program work but does not meet international visitors at the airport. These four individuals are assisted by two secretaries. Miami functions with one officer-level employee and two lower-ranking civil servants. Seattle's staff is similar to that of New Orleans; Honolulu's, to San Francisco.

New York City, with the heaviest load, both in programming and in greeting leaders, has a somewhat larger staff. Four people do most of the programming, assisted by two secretaries, while three individuals who seldom come to the central office—all civil servants, the highest a GS-12 (current salary range, $8,955 to $10,255)—do most of the greeting.

One problem is the fluctuating nature of the workload in the centers. When a two-officer center hits its work peak and has to program fifteen grantees in a single day (four in one morning by a single officer), greeting new grantees is almost an impossibility. The problem has more serious implications for programming than for greeting, which can—but should not as a matter of course—be delegated to an airline representative.

The greeting function, performed by either the program officer who rushes to the airport or by the official greeter who is stationed there regularly, is fourfold: to aid with the formalities of entry, to assist in procuring overnight accommodations if necessary, to pass on any information of use to the grantee received from his embassy or the United States Government in Washington, and to facilitate onward travel.

The major arrival problem, particularly for those under the Foreign Leader Program, stems from the inspection services which are thoroughly performed by Public Health, Immigration and Naturali-

tive details of the program, and to explain how the grantee's program would be worked out by one of the contracting agencies. The quarters of the Leaders Branch, while typical of Washington facilities, have hardly been adequate to receive distinguished foreign visitors. This has led to arrangements to meet grantees in hotel lobbies or elsewhere.

If all has gone well and the area officer has not been too busy, he has made arrangements to take the visitor to meet his program officer at the appropriate contract agency, be it the American Council on Education's Committee on Leaders and Specialists, the Governmental Affairs Institute, or the Trade Unions Program Division, Office of International Labor Affairs, the Department of Labor. Often, however, the visitor has been given directions to go by himself to the contract agency. In either case, the area officer has normally got in touch with the program officer ahead of time to make any particular suggestions on the basis of his short conversation with the grantee. Sometimes the grantee has walked into the contract agency unannounced without any prior notification of his arrival.

Enough foreign visitors are arriving in Washington every year to make their reception a major problem. A new Department of State reception center has been established to assume the airport welcoming function, relieving the area officers of this duty. This should ensure that the grantees arriving under the Foreign Leader Program will be accorded treatment in keeping with their position. It has been suggested that each foreign visitor be received at the Washington airport by a counterpart of equal distinction. There will be occasions when high dignitaries should be involved in the reception process, but for the typical foreign leader grantee this would be unnecessary. The time of the visitor's counterparts should be reserved for fruitful discussions and not wasted on ceremonial displays. Efficient reception by well-trained reception center employees is likely to be more appreciated by most foreign leaders than meaningless pleasantries and protocol.

Although the functions assigned to the new reception center by the Department of State were exceedingly limited, it would seem advisable that the center should be used to bypass the Leaders Branch in relation to the arrival process so that grantees could be guided directly to the contract agencies after discussion with center employees. This would allow the area officers in the Leaders Branch to concentrate on monitoring program operations or other supervisory functions and not make the reception center still another bureaucratic layer through which the hapless foreign leader has to thread his way. The Leaders Branch contributes no "red-carpet" aspect to the reception process at present, and the Department's recognition of the visitor can better be given in the form of brief substantive discussions with appropriate Department officers of somewhat higher level than the area officers.

3

Nation-wide Programming

THE DIRECT PARTICIPATION of the Department of State in the nation-wide programming of foreign leaders has been minimal since 1954 when programming became the responsibility of the three "contract agencies": the Governmental Affairs Institute, the Committee on Leaders and Specialists of the American Council on Education, and the Office of International Labor Affairs, Department of Labor. Even after the designation of the contract agencies to program foreign leaders and specialists, however, a unit now known as the Voluntary Leaders Branch of the Leaders and Specialists Division, Office of Cultural Exchange, continued to render assistance in programming "groups and individual leaders coming to the United States under the auspices of individuals or organizations other than the United States Government, . . . when they are deemed to contribute to achieving the objectives of the Educational Exchange Program."

Currently, approximately nine-tenths of the visitors coming under the Foreign Leader Program are programmed by one of the three contract agencies. There are those who feel that enough flexibility should be possible in the program so that a few individuals with an exceptional understanding of American life could be allowed substantial freedom to arrange their own programs and to pursue their individual interests outside normal channels. It is certain that the number capable of following such a pattern would be small, but the value of such an alternative is more important than the number of those who might be involved. If administrative problems can be worked out, the idea should be tested.

THE PROGRAM AREAS OF THE THREE CONTRACT AGENCIES

Division of responsibility among the three contract agencies handling leaders is determined on the basis of professional competence and interest. The Governmental Affairs Institute is "responsible for leaders in Governmental affairs, political science, journalism, radio and television, who are primarily interested in civic, political, governmental and international activities." The American Council on Education is "responsible for leaders primarily interested in education, fine arts, cultural activities, youth organizations, social work and related activities." The Office of International Labor Affairs, Department of Labor, is "responsible for leaders primarily interested in trade unions, labor-management relations, working conditions, etc."

It is obvious from these statements that there may be times when assignment could be made to any one of the three agencies. This is useful, within limits, as a means of making optimum use of available staffs so long as good judgment is exercised by the assigning area officers in the Leaders Branch of the Department of State. Within the contract agencies, groups or individual foreign leaders are assigned by the head of the agency to program officers on the basis of professional specialization and the current workload of individual officers, occasionally taking into account the level of the leader and the area from which he comes. It is possible, through sensitive assignment and the chance possession of the right background by a program officer, for a leader to be programmed with great understanding by a man who knows the relevant professional field, the visitor's homeland, and the nature of his leadership role. Under pressure when the appropriate program officer may not be available—or if the visitor's background does not happen to coincide with that of any of the program officers—programming is less effective.

PROGRAMMING THE FOREIGN LEADER

Present problems in programming foreign leaders stem from many causes beyond the contract agencies' control. The objectives of the Foreign Leader Program influence the selection and notification processes, and thereby the suitability and adaptability of the leaders for the experiences which the Leader Program can provide. The selection and notification processes influence the quality of the visitors, the degree of orientation provided overseas, and the care with which information on the individual grantee is prepared and forwarded to the Department of State. The Department's relatively modest role of leadership in relationship to the field, stemming in part from these factors as well as the constant rotation of its personnel and their immersion in administrative detail, tends to weaken central control of the flow of leaders. This situation creates occasional overloads and makes effective programming difficult.

Even if the grantee has a personality and interests that fit within the limitations of the program, and all other steps prior to programming have been adequately carried out, "the whole business of working out a program is a nervous affair so far as the program officer is concerned," as one official interviewed put it. Most officers function on the assumption that the leader feels that "it is his program and you are here to help him see what he wants to see in America." If in the process of balancing the program between professional interests and things the grantee wants to see in addition, the program officer uncovers distortions in the visitor's view of America, he may proffer suggestions for experiences and information which would tend to correct such misconceptions—for example, in the fields of labor or race relations. Typically, the program is a combination of the visitor's wishes and the host-agency's suggestions.

A few of the major problems arising from present practices in the contract agencies include: scheduling too many stopovers in a single 60-day, or shorter, trip; sending leaders to too many large urban centers; programming too many leaders to the same cities at the same time; encouraging too many strictly professional visits; failing too often to take into account the need for periods of rest and reflection; a reluctance to schedule the leader for a pre-trip orientation experience or a terminal seminar to provide a framework for interpreting the American scene; setting up a schedule which necessitates too many nights in hotels and too few nights in private homes; and a general failure to lay on the line during program discussions the difficulties and frustrations which are almost certain to accompany sixty days of travel about the United States.

The role of the program officer is often one of arranging what the visitor wants to do within a tight time schedule, but such a program may fail to take into account a decline of interest as "professional experiences begin to come out of the grantee's ears" and as his stamina proves to be less than superhuman. Traveling in unfamiliar territory is more difficult than in an environment one knows and likes. Contacts in an unfamilar language require more concentration than those in one's native tongue. Understanding behavior patterns in an alien culture is more difficult than analyzing the mores of one's own community. The program officer must restrict the program to tolerable limits and not treat the visit as a "once in a lifetime affair" which necessitates the leader's doing everything there is to do in the United States within sixty days or less.

If the proper orientation has been given overseas, the program officer can enforce wholesome limitations which are not designed to prevent the visitor from seeing the reality of American life but rather to make it possible for him to appreciate such reality without feeling oppressed. Relative freedom of action must be retained by the visitor in determining which of several major aspects of American life he may wish to explore. But few visiting leaders are in a position to determine the best methods by which they can conduct this exploration in a limited amount of time. This requires a perspective no single foreign visitor can have.

It is not fair to say that after a visitor has seen one major American city he has seen them all. Washington, Philadelphia, New York, Boston, Cleveland, Chicago, Minneapolis, and New Orleans have distinct personalities. But viewed briefly and without orientation, there may appear to be little difference between professors at Harvard and the University of Chicago, between the bars in New York and New Orleans, between the views of labor leaders in Philadelphia and Cleveland, between businessmen in one part of America and another, and between the second-best hotels in any of these cities. Perhaps one must visit three to five such cities to arrive at this conclusion but scarcely more. Large urban centers are usually too complex for the typical foreign leader to come to grips with in less than a week, even when the leader is fresh in mind and body.

Too often when the visitor arrives in another large city he wants nothing more than to escape into anonymity and rest. He could become more refreshed and more in a mood for reflection if he were to find himself in a quiet resort area, possibly with a few other leader visitors with whom he could exchange views informally. One or two such experiences in the course of a visit might be useful and would reduce the inclination to use Chicago, New York, or New Orleans stopovers as rest stops. In view of individual differences, the pause should not be institutionalized to the point of becoming an absolute requirement, or of holding formal discussions. It should be planned sufficiently in advance so the leader may decide several days ahead whether or not he wants to take advantage of the opportunity. There are some for whom too much time for rest might bring on homesickness. And a few might fear that the purpose of the pause was to abbreviate the time available to look into American problems.

Informally, some thoughtful local sponsors, upon discovering that a leader is fatigued or bored, may make special arrangements after his arrival to permit him to visit some restful nearby resort for a brief respite. Regularly, some local program sponsors relieve the pressure of the trip by scheduling a half day to a day of free time for the visitor out of every three days. But, more often, the grantee is likely to be visiting the same old counterparts, some of whom have already talked with too many visitors.

There remains a practically virgin territory to which the foreign leaders are seldom exposed—middle-sized and smaller communities in which the foreign visitor is of interest and to which he can contribute new ideas, communities small enough for the visitor to study and comprehend. While some progress has been made toward opening up new resource areas, the statistics prove that real dispersion of leaders is yet to be accomplished. While this failure stems in part from the proclivities of the visitors to travel to the big cities with whose names they are most familiar, in even greater measure it is the result of a failure of the contract agencies to organize themselves to open up and use new resources, largely because of a lack of funds and staff, to take the initiative in routing the leader where he will get the most individual attention which will stimulate his interest and allow him to see and exchange ideas with Americans who are eager for such exchanges. The contract agencies do not have sufficient knowledge of even the cities and the institutions upon which they now depend. This is not to suggest that the present cities have been exhausted and should be severely cut back or dropped from itineraries altogether. In most instances, only certain resources within these cities are continuously overtaxed, while others are ignored. Visitors may be sent to cities at times when the resources that are available are in slack periods of operation and not prepared to deal adequately with the visitor.

Admittedly there are problems for the contract agencies as they attempt to expand their operations into smaller communities. It may sometimes be difficult to find local program sponsors with sufficient sophistication to appeal to the visiting leaders. Suffice it to say, an interested, albeit provincial, American may make a better impression on a foreign leader than a bored urban intellectual. There are alert college graduates in most American communities who are intelligent enough and possess sufficient knowledge to discuss local, state, and national problems in a context which should be of interest to the intelligent and receptive foreign visitor. It may be that the visit will also spark new local interest in foreign affairs.

FUTURE ROLE OF THE CONTRACT AGENCIES

Suggestions for improving the operations of the contract agencies range from the more modest and cautious suggestion of strengthening current procedures to returning the programming function to the Department of State. The following analysis is based on the belief that, given the expenditure of sufficient time, energy, and money, the Foreign Leader Program could be programmed successfully either inside or outside the Department of State. However, if the fundamental goal is to provide the visitor with an objective look at reality, there is much to be said, both psychologically and practically, for leaving most programming to private agencies somewhat removed from the political concerns and responsibilities of governmental institutions.

It must be recognized that it would be possible for the Department of State to refrain from the "hard sell" approach. It is also possible for private citizens to be chauvinistic. However, it must be realized that a program directly under Department of State control tends to be suspect. Nor must the Department forget the value of interesting the American people in foreign affairs and stimulating private organizations to concern themselves with its programs. Without discounting the need for leadership and assistance from the Department of State, the stimulation of individual initiative unlocks potentials which a strictly governmental operation can scarcely equal. This does not mean we must forsake ultimate federal control and guidance; private individuals require assistance and general direction from the Government.

Returning all programming to the Department would be a traumatic change, revolution rather than evolution. It would have an immediately unfavorable impact upon the conduct of the program. In view of the present predilection for considerable Foreign Service officer staffing of Department of State operations concerned with the Foreign Leader Program, one must ask if the Foreign Service is currently staffed to assume the responsibility for programming which would involve a heavy additional burden and require a detailed knowledge of program opportunities in the United States. Or are the Department and the United States Information Agency prepared to absorb present program officers in the contract agencies into their respective personnel services? Could the Department attract top quality civil servants to programming positions when career preference in the Department is given largely to Foreign Service officers? There is no certainty that the answer would be "yes" to any of these questions.

In view of the recommendation made earlier to organize special programs for a small number of leaders, the Department of State should program a limited number of these visitors now handled by the contract agencies, not as a cure-all but to maintain expertise and to ensure that the special purposes for which such leaders are brought can be given special and direct attention. If the visit is viewed as a substitute for a State visit or if the position of the individual is such that he must be dealt with separately—even though he does not meet the requirements of the Foreign Leader Program—there may be real merit in making such a visitor the direct charge of the Department of State.

Such a visit is likely to be more expensive than the visit of a typical foreign leader. It is likely to require special planning and greater care in escorting the participant about the United States. The Department's prestige can on occasion unlock doors not responsive to the knock of private citizens. If such visits were handled through regular channels, they would rob time from the programming of more typical leaders. It is also possible that the Department could not communicate sufficiently to private agencies the purposes of the visit or the problems of the visitor so that the visit could be fully productive.

The number of special purpose visits would not need to be large—perhaps no more than 10 per cent of the leaders coming to America in a single year. These visitors should be programmed by the Department after the establishment and careful staffing of a new Special Programs Branch in the Leaders and Specialists Division. Direct intervention of the Department of State is no guarantee, however, that all such visitors will be more satisfied than if they were programmed in the contract agencies.

IMPROVING CONTRACT AGENCY PROGRAMMING

Further improvement in the programming and supervision of leaders by the contract agencies can be achieved by giving increasing attention to the following problem areas: (1) relations of the contract agencies with the Department of State; (2) relations within and among contract agencies; (3) in-service training of program officers; (4) facilities for programming; (5) fluctuation of the workload; (6) relations of the contract agency representatives with the field overseas; (7) biographic information on grantees; (8) pre-trip orientation of leaders; (9) development of community resources; (10) relations of contract agencies with local program sponsors; and (11) entertainment and emergency allowances.

A representative program officer has said that the contract agencies are not sure what the Department of State wants them to do or how well the Department thinks they are doing their work. This statement is indicative of some failure on the part of the Department to assume a proper role of leadership. Relations between the Department and the contract agencies have focused more on program emergencies than on the regular discussion of general problems. Recent steps toward utilization of conferences to bring together departmental personnel and the program officers of the contract agencies have proved helpful. Conferences should be continued on a semiannual basis, between workload peaks, for the frank exchange of views on a broad range of common concerns.

The steps being taken within the Department of Labor to improve liaison with the Department of State may prove helpful in the long run. The increasing number of labor leaders to be brought under the Foreign Leader Program may require more immediate and higher level action to bring about a substantial broadening of the programs for labor leaders to meet the objectives of the Leader Program.

While formal staff meetings within the contract agencies for the discussion of program problems are not ideal vehicles for exchanging ideas or making suggestions for improvement, regular sessions of program officers with planned agendas and sufficient time for thorough consideration of selected questions would be better than *ad hoc* discussions at lunch or weekly half-hour meetings, which must be more concerned with immediate operations than with more long-range matters. Program officers spend a good deal of their time operating by themselves, with less contact with their fellow officers than seems advisable. This lack of contact is understandable during the peak influx of visitors, but it is questionable whether communication is any better in slack times.

There seems to be little regular or planned communication among the contract agencies. As a result, they may learn only informally— if a program officer happens to have a friend in another agency— about improvements initiated elsewhere. During the summer of 1960 one agency was considering altering its facilities for the reception and programming of leaders and had not even considered visiting the other contract agencies to see their facilities or to get suggestions which might be incorporated in its own planning. There is apparently little coordination among the contract agencies in scheduling visits to local communities, so it is possible for an overload to strike the local sponsor at a given time.

There is little exchange of knowledge about community resources. Each contract agency gathers its own information and tends to make exclusive use of it. The establishment of the staff of the National Council for Community Services to International Visitors at the Washington International Center and the shift of these community services from the sheltering wing of the Governmental Affairs Institute may help to meet this problem. Occasional interagency staff meetings and some coordination of itineraries might resolve other difficulties.

Program officers tend to be persons who might otherwise be members of college and university faculties, drawn into the programming of foreign leaders because of the interesting work and favorable salaries compared to academic pay for comparable training and work. The type of job they are doing, however, has existed for only a short time. The opportunities for advancement appear uncertain. It seems likely that few program officers would consider this type of work a life-time career. Since some turnover is likely and there is no specific preparatory course for such a job, devices for in-service training appear to be a necessity. Regular staff meetings, discussions among contract agencies staffs, conferences with representatives of the Department of State and typical local program sponsors, opportunities to travel abroad to visit embassies and leaders, plus at least one swing around the United States as an escort officer, or a reasonably equivalent experience, would all be helpful training devices. Courses on cross-cultural relations at the Foreign Service Institute would be of value. Time for in-service training, however, will require additional personnel or fewer foreign leaders. If the workload were tolerable, the opportunities for in-service training increased, and the program stable, it seems likely that program officers would tend to become "professionals" and would be willing to remain for longer periods of time.

Facilities for the reception of visitors and programming vary greatly among the three contract agencies. Some efforts need to be made to bring all reception and programming facilities at least up to the Governmental Affairs Institute level, which is currently the best among the three and the only one which is reasonably adequate.

The leader should not be thrown into the informality of American life until he has been conditioned for it. A leader cannot be handed a cafeteria tray until he understands that this is typical Americana and not an affront to his personal dignity. His secretary's brief case cannot be inspected coming out of the Library of Congress until he realizes that all Americans are subjected to such surveillance. So long as his basic needs are provided for and he is given rapid transportation so as not to waste his time, he must rub elbows with Americans and learn their customs. This relatively democratic treatment should not begin, however, until there has been sufficient time to sit down with the leader and to explain the nature of the trip and the American scene—when he is free of official duties and has his mind on his trip.

The fluctuation in the workload of the program officers under present stringent staffing patterns is unfortunate, bringing the poorest programming during the times of the year when the greatest numbers of visitors are arriving in America. While it will be impossible to stabilize the flow completely, the Department must give constant attention to minimizing the variations. It may even be necessary to reduce the total number of visitors. If this is to be avoided, additional funds for increasing the number of program officers will be necessary. If in-service training opportunities are to be established for contract agency personnel and if time is to be set aside for contract agency personnel to learn to know community resources better and to expand the number of communities to be utilized, agencies must be staffed so that program officers may give more attention to such experiences.

Relations of the contract agencies with the field overseas are usually quite indirect. One long-time program officer complained that he had been an "apprentice" for many years but had yet to become a "journeyman." Although he dealt continuously with leaders from abroad, he had never been abroad. Funds are needed so that several program officers from each of the contract agencies can be sent overseas to talk with embassy representatives and to meet with alumni of the Leader Program in their home environment. If money for this cannot be provided in Department contracts with the agencies, it should be sought from private foundations. Not only could the program officers communicate their problems rather directly to the cultural affairs officers or others involved in exchange programs, but they could better understand the reasons for shortcomings in the overseas processes. Another useful device would be the routing of cultural affairs officers to the contract agencies for discussions when they are in Washington. While the contract agencies occasionally participate in the orientation of cultural affairs officers, this is not a regular practice. Perhaps this is because of stringent staffing patterns and the excessive workload during peak periods; it may also stem from forgetfulness or a lack of understanding by the United States Information Agency regarding the possible value of such contacts.

While the Department of State is exploring the possibility of making more biographic information available to the contract agencies so that they may program each individual leader more intelligently, it is likely that sufficient information can never be put down in black and white and forwarded to contract agency personnel. With the reorganization of the Bureau of Educational and Cultural Affairs, however, there may be more time for informal telephone calls to paraphrase necessary information for the use of program officers. It would also help if cultural affairs officers were more adequately alerted to the biographic data problem before assignment overseas. More orderly selection and departure of grantees from overseas would be of assistance. There appears to be no one clear-cut solution to knowing each individual grantee sufficiently well to do the best possible job of programming, but steps can be taken to fill present gaps in biographic information.

The occasional failure of the foreign leader to receive adequate orientation during the course of his programming in the contract agencies stems from many causes. The tendency to treat the visitors as though they were all equal to planning their trips, until they show neither the inclination nor the ability to do so, stems from the "freedom of action" concept. As a result, some leaders are unreceptive to suggestions, resent the necessity of spending time to plan programs, and often pretend to know more and to be better travelers than is the case. In turn, the program officers, placed in a position of treating visitors with deference and without definite authority, allow some of their charges to become rather freewheeling. The workload often provides a ready excuse for not harassing the leader with details about the trip. The fact that most program officers have not lived through a visit themselves makes them less certain how firm they should be in making suggestions or in telling the leader of the assorted problems he may face. Indeed, it may be that few of the program officers fully understand the value of the orientation process which can set a frame of reference within which the foreign leader may operate throughout his trip. The leader is in a hurry to "get on with it." He may show impatience if he is not soon put in consultation with colleagues. Some consultation is arranged during the Washington stay, but colleagues usually talk more of substantive matters than about the nature of the trip the visitor is to undertake. So the program officer needs more time for contact with the leaders. This may necessitate more funds for entertainment if the program officer is to spend additional time with the visitor. Orientation requires time and a relaxed atmosphere for the program officer to get to know the grantee well enough to do an adequate job of orientation.

One hears again and again of the visiting leader who arrived in a city the day after an event that would have been interesting to him or who had to leave the day before it occurred. More adequate attention should be devoted to gathering information on special events and knowing the dates when local sponsors cannot usefully receive visitors. Some progress is now being made along these lines.

Another problem is the desire of the grantee to change his program en route as he finds he has planned too much or becomes interested in some new aspect of American life. Local program sponsors occasionally pass on such information to the next city to be visited. Sometimes, on an emergency basis, this may be desirable. It would seem preferable, however, for the contract agency to make a careful check about every two weeks with whatever local sponsor may then be in charge of the visitor to discuss the possibility of program revision. Advice based on this information should be forwarded to local program sponsors yet to be visited.

Relations of the contract agencies with the local program sponsors are largely conducted by telephone or letter. A program sponsor may visit the contract agencies when in Washington for some other purpose. Contract agency representatives have visited a few communities and talked with some local sponsors. Representatives of the Department of State and the contract agencies have met with local sponsors in regional or state-wide conferences on funds provided by the Department. Such contacts should be encouraged. Funds should be provided for increasing the number of regional conferences and for permitting program officers to make more field trips to exchange views with local program sponsors. Agency officers upon occasion do serve as escorts of leaders in Washington. The experience of living through a tour and the opportunity to meet local sponsors should enable a program officer to do a more realistic job. If staffing of contract agencies can become less stringent, it would be useful for all program officers to have the opportunity early in their service and occasionally later, to act as an escort for a leader's tour of the United States.

The need for allowances for modest hospitality and emergency expenditures which may arise during a leader's trip is pressing. It is foolish to do a poor job of programming a visitor for want of several dollars for entertainment and discussions under informal conditions. It is unfortunate for a leader to become upset if he loses money en route and is required to pay it back. In each case, the benefit of the trip may be lost for want of modest funds at the proper moment. The resistance of the Congress on this issue requires some reconsideration so that the contract agencies can accomplish the ends for which they were established. It would seem desirable to give the agencies sufficient funds to provide for essential entertainment and emergency needs both in Washington and in the field. Control of this process by the Department of State would be cumbersome; control by local sponsors in the field, too difficult to administer. The contract agencies should have knowledge of the over-all pattern of a visit and understand the circumstances in which the use of such funds would be most advisable. Seeking such funds through programming of other types of visitors only overloads program officers and takes their attention away from the leaders and specialists. The contract agencies must have these funds if they are to establish a program of quality. Further exploration of the problem would be required before a firm recommendation could be made regarding the amount of such funds needed. It would seem that $20,000 a year for such purposes would be a bare minimum; $25,000 would be more nearly adequate. If the contract agencies are to be trusted with the vital processes of programming and supervising the trips of foreign leaders, they should be given the wherewithal and flexibility to meet their responsibilities. Local program sponsors cannot always find financial support to arrange meetings which would be most productive for the leaders. It is unfortunate that in many instances dinners are given because the donor expects to gain something individually, perhaps in a business or social way. How much better it would be if the leader could be programmed for an experience because he and the United States Government might benefit. To accomplish these more worthwhile ends, it is well not to be "penny wise and pound foolish."

PER DIEM ALLOWANCES

Per diem allowances for most foreign leaders have recently been increased from $17 to $20, with no more than 10 per cent of the leaders given $25 per day. There have been suggestions that the per diem allowance should be increased to a maximum of $50. A first reaction to this latter figure is that it might create more problems than it would solve. Too high a standard of living might tend to separate the leader from the average American. Many leaders from underdeveloped lands already find it possible to save enough money to purchase American appliances to take home; thus they live on considerably less that their $20 per day. But even $20 per day will not allow much financial leeway for most leaders unless home hospitality is offered enough of the time to cut costs substantially on a number of days. Many of the leaders cannot bring funds out of their countries and are completely dependent upon the money they receive here. A number live less well during their trip than they do at home.

On tour, even with special rates in some hotels, the cost of normal food, local transportation, and laundry (plus cleaning and pressing) can easily consume $20, without allowing much for the purchase of newspapers or periodical literature. Little is left for cultural and other recreational events. Fortunately, some cities are less expensive than others. Some have pointed out that $25 might be a more respectable amount for all leader visitors, allowing them to stay in better hotels, to eat more adequately, to attend additional events for which tickets have to be purchased, to use faster transportation with less waste of time, and to put a little bit aside to take something home.

It is fair to say that the new $20 per diem rate will ease the pressure, but there are many benefits that would accrue from increasing the rate to $25. Anything more would seem unreasonable for the typical leader in view of the fact that he will receive some home hospitality. There are some advantages in encouraging and enabling him to buy his own tickets to events he wishes to see. In addition, the mementos of the trip which he takes home are not of negligible significance. They become conversation pieces that convey many ideas about America to the leader's friends and relatives. The Department and the Congress could do worse than to encourage this use of some per diem funds.

GROUP PROGRAMS

Although the discussion to this point has emphasized the programming of individual leaders, groups of journalists, educators, parliamentarians, and young political leaders have been an increasingly important aspect of the Leader Program. Some of these group efforts have been quite successful; others, near disasters. Questions arise, therefore, regarding the wisdom of the growing emphasis upon group programs.

There are good reasons why group programming has been used. The greater the number of leaders in a group—up to a point—the more worthwhile it appears to important figures in American life to give interviews to the visitors. Top political figures can rarely afford to give time to an individual leader unless there is a special reason for such a conversation. Quite often, however, they are willing to participate in some form of group conference. More visitors can be handled by the contract agencies with somewhat less effort than if the leaders are programmed individually. Since group arrangements are worked out in considerable detail before the arrival of the group—as opposed to the practice of waiting to talk with an individual—the scheduling can be done at a convenient time and used to balance the program officer's workload.

Coming as a member of a group tends to relieve the individual leader of any necessity to explain why he, personally, is accepting a tour sponsored by a foreign government. A further advantage to the leader is that as a member of a group he can talk over his experiences regularly with his fellow observers and cross-check impressions continuously. Leaders in groups are less likely to become lonely, and they are guaranteed some status by the very fact that groups are accorded special attention.

On the other hand, group contacts have tended to be more ceremonial than individual conversations. While some groups have been interested in substantive discussions, others have seemed to view the tour as a paid vacation. Selection has not seemed to be as careful as in the case of a single leader. A member of a group can have some individual programming but much of the time he must follow a common pattern, sometimes one in which he is not personally interested.

Many of the problems of the past have stemmed from poor selection and orientation. One group of educators arrived believing that they were to be programmed separately around the United States. A group of journalists came for a special conference believing they were here over the weekend only to find they had been invited to a ten-day conference. Some of the problems have arisen from the "crash" nature of a project—after a serious reaction has occurred abroad and there has been an effort to achieve quick impact in a particular profession.

This experience suggests that group programming should be done with greater discretion than in the past. The grand tour concept has not always worked badly but it has failed on a number of occasions. Such tours can be usefully conducted for only those groups with a serious substantive interest (and when no wives are included). The members of each group should be carefully screened for general suitability, and careful orientation on the nature of the experience ought to be provided overseas by the American Embassy. The problems of the local sponsors—not always made clear in formal reports—are difficult to exaggerate when an ill-chosen uninterested vacationing group hits town. It is doubtful if such groups have gained any increase in respect for the United States, its citizens, or themselves.

Of the suggestions made above for improvement in nation-wide programming, no one specifically concerns the number of points visited by leaders programmed individually during a 60-day tour or the amount of time which the individual visitor might usefully spend in a single city. Such decisions depend upon the needs of the particular visitor and the resources of a specific city. Generally speaking, the rather frenetic nature of the present program can be substantially alleviated by programming leaders to fewer cities. If there are fewer stopovers, each stop can be more carefully selected by both visitor and program officer. Giving the foreign leader time to settle momentarily in a particular city will provide him with the opportunity to learn more about that type of community so that he will be able to go beyond narrow professional contacts or mere sightseeing. Of course, such a recommendation must be dependent upon progress toward the more careful selection of leaders and a sincere desire on the part of the United States that they come for positive purposes. It may well be that some of the visitors to be programmed directly by the Department of State can best be dealt with by providing general contacts in American communities, but this would not be true in many cases. For the typical foreign leader, motion must not be confused with education. If there is diversity in America, there is also much that is the same in its various parts. If the leader has a proper overview of the American scene, he may profit by surveying fewer points of interest at greater depth. At best sixty days is time for sampling and savoring, not for wolfing the country down whole.

4

Orientation and Cross-cultural Communication

EACH INDIVIDUAL TENDS TO INTERPRET what he observes in relation to past experience and knowledge. Actions taken or values held by American citizens can be understood only when seen in the broader frame of reference of American society. Any segment of American life taken out of context and interpreted in relation to the culture of another society will yield a distorted meaning.

It is conceivable that an intelligent and honest foreign leader, without orientation on American society and with the best of intentions, could observe the American scene for forty-five to sixty days and have a more negative feeling toward it than he might have had without any observation. It is less conceivable that the realistic foreign leader who sees Americans for what they actually are—including their shortcomings—will actively dislike them, although he may not agree with all he sees and may find many American practices undesirable for quick or easy transfer to his homeland.

Bringing foreign leaders to the United States without providing general orientation is a bit like playing Russian roulette. While one can say, "We are not that different," or "They must have read something about us," there is need to consider whether some form of briefing may not be necessary for most if not all foreign leaders. Indeed, some form of orientation would be useful for most Americans before they began a tour of their own country if they were to get the most out of the trip.

THE WASHINGTON INTERNATIONAL CENTER

The Washington International Center was established at the request of the Government in 1950 as a project of the American Council on Education.[1] Its 26-member staff, ranging from director to janitor, receives guidance from a special 13-member advisory committee on policy. Currently, the center's educational programs seek attainment of the following five objectives:

1. To help the visitor make a satisfactory personal adjustment to his new cultural environment through discussion of unfamiliar customs, use of facilities and services, location and arrangement of streets, buildings and points of interest, and sources of further personal help and information.
2. To present to the visitor a descriptive analysis of cultural patterns and institutions in American life and to show how they inter-relate, thus establishing the larger cultural frame-of-reference for his understanding of new technical knowledge.
3. To help the visitor understand the forms and processes through which social and cultural change takes place, as he observes its course and development in a different society from his own. . . .
4. To help the visitor appreciate the role and influence of individuals and groups in shaping and modifying institutions and policies in a free society. Here, the United States is regarded not as a model but as a living laboratory in which problems of democratic life can be observed, tested and openly discussed. (This objective can be kept free of any propaganda motive so long as . . . the examination of life here is open to free inquiry and objective analysis.)
5. To create through mutual discussion of cultural differences and common problems a greater sense of mutual confidence and shared responsibility for national and international progress.

---

[1] Washington International Center was operated as a project of the American Council on Education for ten years. As of July 1, 1961, the center is now operated by the newly formed Meridian House Foundation, made up of several organizations working independently in the international field, at 1630 Crescent Place N.W., Washington 9, D.C.

In short, the programs are intended to "communicate something of the wholeness or organic nature of American life and society." In pointing out how this is accomplished, one of the International Center's publications declares, "Leaders, specialists, and technical experts from all over the world come to the Center to further their acquaintance with the United States before they pursue their individual goals of study and travel as guests of the United States Government." The pamphlet indicates that the "program speakers may be officials from various departments of the Government; they may be professors from such universities as George Washington, Howard, American, or Georgetown; they may be professional economists or labor union leaders; they may be officials from any one of such national organizations as the United States Chamber of Commerce, the American Civil Liberties Union, the National Catholic Welfare Conference, or from such national institutions as the Library of Congress or the National Gallery of Art." It is explained that through this program "visitors gain new perspectives of the United States—its physical and economic growth, social changes in its history, the system of government and role of political parties, the American family and its health and welfare, religious life and institutions, economic trends and development, public and private school education, civil liberties and race relations, and foreign policy."

Maps, films, and charts are used to enliven the International Center's lecture-discussions. Background booklets on lecture topics, such as education, government, and labor unions, are available for more leisurely perusal at a later time, along with general materials on such matters as Lincoln, music, sports, the land and its people, which give an overview of how Americans live and work.

Although leaders are listed first among the three categories of foreign visitors serviced by the Washington International Center, they make up no more than 5 per cent of the approximately 5,000 individuals participating in center programs in the course of a year. As a matter of fact, apparently fewer than one-third of the visiting leaders programmed by the American Council on Education and the Governmental Affairs Institute take part in center programs. Almost no labor visitors here under the Foreign Leader Program have been scheduled to the center by the Department of Labor in recent years. Former leader participants in center programs have written center staff members a number of letters indicating their happiness with participation in its orientation programs.

Many program officers in the contract agencies express little interest in scheduling foreign leaders to the Washington International Center or in finding out through first-hand observation what happens there. When leaders arrive at a contract agency they have normally never heard of the center. They have not been prepared for the possibility of devoting some time to formal orientation before embarking on their tour. They are sometimes scarcely willing to talk with substantive experts in Washington about their professional interests before taking off on the grand tour.

Not all the blame for the small percentage of leaders utilizing the center can be placed upon those who brief the leaders overseas, or upon the contract agencies. If a leader is sent to the center, he is likely to find himself feeling a bit out of place in orientation sessions, sometimes surrounded by persons of considerably less status who are traveling under other exchange programs. He may find himself in a lecture group with as many as thirty individuals, in which a relatively stereotyped program is presented which may not be addressed to his particular interests or needs. Even if the leader has been fortunate and is scheduled with his peers for a special two-day seminar, the instructor may lecture instead of encouraging discussion.

Nor can the center be held responsible for all of its shortcomings. Arrival dates of foreign leaders are often uncertain; thus, special programs cannot always be planned. Discussion may be made difficult because of the diverse backgrounds of the foreign leaders and language difficulties, which can be only partially overcome by simultaneous translation of the lecturer's remarks when no provision is made for simultaneous translation of remarks of the other participants.

Add to all of these limiting factors the additional pressure on the schedules of the leaders when—beginning with fiscal year 1957—visits from most areas were limited to sixty rather than ninety days, and the time allocated for orientation generally cut from five to two days. In five days perhaps the center could begin to explain the American scene. How much can be communicated in a two-day period?

IMPROVING THE ORIENTATION PROCESS

In view of the need for some knowledge of America before observing it directly, what foreign leaders should receive formal orientation before beginning their tour? There are many in the contract agencies who would argue that the present arrangement is satisfactory. Others argue for a higher precentage of participation, and there are a few who believe that every foreign leader should take part in such orientation.

Much of the argument for maintaining the present level of assignment to the orientation program is based on the nature of the leaders now selected for the program, their lack of preparation overseas for the possibility of orientation in Washington, the difficulty of scheduling special and separate programs for leaders, and the feeling of many leaders that they do not need such orientation. Unfortunately, this situation does not meet the minimum requirements to enable many foreign leaders to understand the American scene.

Those who would send all foreign leaders through formal orientation recognize the difficulties of cross-cultural understanding, but fail to take into account individual differences. They may not be aware of some of the limitations which will prevent such a program from being adapted to the needs of every leader. Some leaders who might be programmed directly by the Department of State might not be interested in understanding the total American scene. Whatever orientation is given them should probably be of an informal nature, perhaps by escorts en route. There may be a few leaders who have already devoted some time to the study of American society and are more or less experts on the subject. Furthermore, there are language complications; individuals who are assigned a competent staff interpreter might be able to receive background briefing en route with less effort than in a formal orientation program.

Whether all other leaders should be programmed through a formal orientation program will depend on the nature of their overseas orientation and the quality of the program to be offered them. If formal orientation is to be given greater emphasis, and it seems that it should be, the original invitation to the foreign leader should note this as a regular part of the program, and the orientation program should be designed to meet the needs of the leaders.

The question then arises, in view of the 60- rather than 90-day limitation, how long should formal orientation last? Is two days enough, as some believe? Would five days provide a more realistic period? Or some longer time? There can be little doubt that a large amount of subject matter can be presented by lecturers in a two-day period. The difficulty with this approach is that the program is liable to be over for some foreign leaders before the first culture shock has worn off. Such a pace of presentation allows little possibility for discussion. If the orientation program is to bring some involvement of the foreign leader and allow some time for reflection, something closer to five days appears to be a more useful period. A longer conference might cut too heavily into the travel time or become boring to a high percentage of the visitors. It would be better to experiment with a five-day program and do it well before moving toward any further extension.

If the program is to be returned to a five-day basis, should the foreign leaders be programmed with exchangees of other programs or should they be handled separately? Ideally, perhaps, the leaders should sit in separate sessions. This would recognize their status and enable their instructors to address themselves to questions which would be especially relevant to leaders. There are several months during the year when traffic of leaders is so low, approximately from November through March, that separate sessions might seem unreasonable. Much is to be said, however, for separate scheduling even at such times. If the teaching staff and funds are available, separation should be maintained, even with small groups of no more than two or three leaders. The smaller the class, the greater the possibility of informal exchange of ideas. Separate and special attention for leader participants will allow the programming agency, the local program sponsors, and the escort-interpreter to know the individual leader's personality and views before the start of the study tour.

There is some question regarding the position of the instructors. Should they be regular members of the center staff? Should they be guest experts brought in to lead discussions on particular topics? Or should they be leading specialists brought in for periods of a year on rotation to conduct such discussions? Presently some discussions are conducted by regular staff members, while special experts are brought in on a one-morning or one-afternoon basis from the Washington area for discussion of other topics. The presence of regular staff personnel lends continuity to the program, while the use of consultants from the Washington area injects an expertise which could not be easily attracted on a full-time basis. So long as the orientation remains a morning and afternoon session experience, with living quarters for participants and discussion leaders elsewhere, the present staffing pattern is perhaps the best that can be attained.

It would be wise to consider the possibility of holding such orientation discussions at a center where residential accommodations could be provided throughout the orientation program for both instructors and guests. There is little doubt that such an experience would give the participants the opportunity for greater concentration on the task at hand and for the establishment of greater rapport with the American discussion leaders. If experts employed in the Washington area found it more difficult to give up the time to participate in such a program for several days, it might be possible to arrange through national professional associations the selection of outstanding young experts in appropriate fields to live in residence at such a center for a year to conduct the formal seminars for foreign leaders and to participate in more informal discussions. They could receive short assists from local experts who could be obtained for single appearances. This type of program would be somewhat expensive, but the expense would be worthwhile. Meridian House, 1630 Crescent Place, N.W., to which the Washington International Center has now moved, does not provide facilities for such a residence center.

The final problem to be considered is the nature of the auspices under which the orientation program should function. Should it be run directly by the Government, contracted out directly to a special organization created to carry out such orientation, or should it be contracted out to an existing educational organization? If the program is to be education, and is to be received by the grantees as education, the orientation program can hardly be run directly by any Government agency. It seems unlikely that a specially created organization would have sufficient prestige to handle such a program.

Therefore, something in the nature of the present relationship of the State Department to the orientation program should be maintained, with an organization like the American Council on Education conducting orientation through some specially created suborgan such as the Washington International Center. This is not to say that the present facilities are adequate. The Washington International Center should be reorganized to provide residential orientation experiences at least for foreign leaders. The fundamental problem is inadequate use of the center and a lack of funds to provide expanded services, not an unwillingness on the part of the Washington International Center or the Amerian Council on Education to provide adequate facilities and programs.

ESCORT-INTERPRETERS

The role of an escort officer may be somewhat different from that of an interpreter, but both functions are often performed in the Foreign Leader Program by a single individual called an escort-interpreter. One basic difference is that the escort officer, while not really adequate for accurate interpretation, can usually carry on a useful conversation with his charge. Another distinction might be that an interpreter would not be responsible for handling financial transactions for the leader as an escort might, but he would be likely to assist the leader in following his schedule and would help adapt it to the visitor's needs as would an escort. Either escort or interpreter might serve as a companion, explaining what the visitor sees in a way that helps to bridge the gap between the visitor's culture and the American milieu.

Escorts are normally provided for all leaders on $25 per diem grants. When such a visitor has a language deficiency, the escort may be called an escort-interpreter and, in that case, must meet the qualifications for interpreter. Both an escort—often a Foreign Service officer from a regional or functional bureau of the Department of State—and one or more interpreters are likely to travel with any high-ranking leader group or delegation. An escort, normally serving as an interpreter as well, may be assigned to a $20 per diem visitor who is an inexperienced traveler or is visiting a region of the United States where special social problems might arise. An interpreter may accompany any $20 per diem visitor who has a language deficiency.

Some proficiency in the English language is considered desirable for leader visitors, but as programs have proceeded in some countries over a period of years English-speaking leaders have been nearly exhausted and the need for interpreters has tended to increase. As the program has scheduled more visits from underdeveloped areas, it has been found that a smaller percentage of these leaders speak English. At present, some 19 staff interpreters from the Department of State Division of Language Services, plus about 30 staff translators,[2] form the core group from which escort-interpreters or interpreters are furnished. Members of this permanent staff have been considered generally effective. In addition, the Division of Language Services signs yearly contracts with some 300 to 350 individuals who have been examined and approved and from whom additional escort-interpreters or interpreters may be provided. As the flow of exchangees rises in peak periods, a high percentage of foreign leaders are accompanied by these contract employees rather than by permanent personnel.

The capability of a number of the contract escort-interpreters to meet the manifold requirements of the program has been seriously questioned by many who are acquainted with this activity. The Division of Language Services is aware of the unevenness in the capabilities of the contractors but finds it impossible in current circumstances to meet all of the demands made upon it with fully qualified personnel. The Department's need for interpreters has increased 2500 per cent in ten years. Supply has not kept pace with demand. As a result, some leaders may be accompanied by an individual who has linguistic ability and a knowledge of the visitor's culture but only a limited knowledge of American society, or one who has linguistic ability and some knowledge of American society but little knowledge of the visitor's culture. Shortages have developed in the course of a year so that an interpreter who did not know the leader's language had to be assigned. The two toured the United States talking in a third language which both knew.

[2] The former primarily interprets orally with people, while the latter normally translates from written copy.

Contract interpreting is a source of uncertain income because the contractor may or may not be called upon in the course of the year. Few really able individuals are attracted by such unstable employment, although the pay ranges from $18 to $30 per day plus $20 per diem with no accounting of spending. Because the leader is introduced to America through the voice and the eyes of the man who accompanies him, any lack of quality among escort-interpreters poses an acute problem.

Some of the contract interpreters tend to assume the status of the high-ranking visitor during their tour with him and behave in a manner that offends program officers in the contract agencies, representatives of local sponsors, and others who meet with the foreign leader for substantive and social purposes. This is not to say that all contract interpreters are unfit. Some are excellent; the majority are adequate. Among those who are considered quite able are some who are not American citizens.

Even the interpreters of real ability, however, do not want to remain in such a trying job for a prolonged period or time. Few contract interpreters are willing to work regularly as escort-interpreters for more than two or three years. If the tour of the United States is tiring to the visiting leader, it is nerve-racking to the interpreter who must accompany the leader almost everywhere he goes. Attrition among the contract interpreters necessitates a constant search for fresh recruits, most of whom receive little formal training before their first tour. Fortunately, the program has been able to obtain from the Division of Language Services some interpreters who have undergone formal training to serve as interpreters for International Cooperation Administration exchange programs, but the Foreign Leader program has no real training program of its own for contract personnel.

QUESTIONS AND RECOMMENDATIONS

Several aspects of the escort-interpreter role have been the subject of considerable debate. Two points of conflict are whether the escort-interpreter should act as the companion or servant of the leader, and whether the escort-interpreter should be a mechanical interpreter or attempt to be a filter through which intercultural distortions can be eliminated.

On the first question, suffice it to say that the foreign leader himself, depending on his personality and the culture from which he comes, will make his own decision and generally should be allowed to set the pattern of the relationship with the interpreter. The leader and his escort-interpreter may be together for ten to fourteen hours a day over a 60-day period, and there must be some mutual respect between the two. But it is unrealistic to expect the leader to accept the average escort-interpreter as a complete equal. Their status is different. The well-adjusted escort-interpreter will follow the lead of the foreign visitor and adapt reasonably to the point on the continuum between companion and servant which is acceptable to the leader. This requires sensitivity and may be a varying relationship in public and private. The escort-interpreter must speak for the foreign leader without demanding the same attention from American program participants as the leader himself.

On the second question, whether the escort-interpreter should be more than a mechanical linguist may depend upon whether he has the ability to play the demanding "filter" role. A number of program officers in the contract agencies and local program sponsors have objected to the assumption of the latter role by men who did it badly. In view of the need, however, to assist the visiting foreign leader to understand what he is seeing and hearing, it is desirable for the competent escort-interpreter to play the filter role and to play it well. Few leaders are so well-trained in cross-cultural communication that this is unnecessary. The solution is not to accept the present lack of ability of some escort-interpreters and to settle for mere linguistic competence. It is rather to improve their capability to meet the interpretive requirements of the program. As important as improved pre-tour orientation seminars might be, especially if most leaders were to participate in them, successful cross-cultural communication would still depend heavily on the skillful escort-interpreter.

There has been some question of whether escorts should be provided not only for special categories of leaders but for all leaders who might desire them, whether all leaders should have to be accompanied by escorts, or whether escorts or interpreters should be supplied only in the most limited numbers. In view of the present shortages of adequate escort-interpreters, any proposal for expanding the use of escorts may seem unrealistic. Additional escorts might be sought, however, among Foreign Service officers in Washington on interim assignment. Some use might be made of Foreign Service officers in the Leaders and Specialists Division or an occasional program officer in a contract agency as an in-service training device. It can be argued that even with competence in English, a foreign leader may not be able to understand or interpret properly what he sees or hears about the American scene.

The present general rule is that $25 per diem visitors are accompanied by an escort regardless of whether they are competent in English. The purpose seems to be more to protect high-ranking visitors from matters of detail or unfortunate experiences than to improve cross-cultural communication. It may be assumed that most visitors of high rank would be accustomed to the performance of some such service and would prefer to have an escort, even though they did not need an interpreter. If, however, proper orientation has been provided beforehand, there are times when these men would prefer to and, on rare occasions, do travel alone.

Generally speaking, it seems preferable that leaders should be accompanied, but there must be room for exceptions. Certainly many individuals programmed directly by the Department of State should be escorted. For the typical foreign leader visitor, it might be well—where an interpreter is not necessary—to offer the escort, explaining his possible value without forcing the leader to accept his services. More effective pre-tour orientation would make such a policy more feasible. Such preparation should make possible a greater degree of freedom during the tour itself. The opportunity to talk informally alone with Americans may be a useful experience for some leaders. The danger that such leaders might leave the United States with distorted impressions can be minimized by their participation in post-tour seminars and the conscious use of informal mid-trip rest and reflection pauses during which the leaders can check their findings with other visitors.

In view of the shortage of capable escort-interpreters during peak program loads, there arises the question of how this problem can be met. There are several possibilities. If the peaks and valleys in the exchange programs can be minimized, or at least those in the Leader Program, additional permanent staff could be recruited by the Division of Language Services of the State Department to meet Leader Program needs. Thus the need for contract escort-interpreters might be somewhat reduced, but the need for some flexibility would not be eliminated. As the Foreign Service continues its new emphasis on language competence, it seems apparent that the percentage of Foreign Service officers—in Washington between overseas assignments or for in-service training at the Foreign Service Institute—with linguistic ability is likely to increase.

Although the skill of interpretation, either consecutive or simultaneous, is different from language knowledge for personal use, it seems likely that progressively more use can be made of Foreign Service officers for the Leader Program. Not only would such officers be able to bring experience in cross-cultural relations and knowledge of a foreign leader's homeland to bear in their temporary service with the program, but they would be able to refresh their own view of the American scene. This is no panacea for the problem of providing capable escort-interpreters, but it is a limited resource of growing usefulness. Progress in this direction, however, will be slow. Foreign Service officers are likely to resist such assignments, and, even if they were willing, the size of the Service needs to be increased if officers are to be made available for such duty.

There is another source of able escort-interpreters, but one which might not be very flexible. Outstanding graduate students or young men with advanced degrees could be selected for one or two years of study in a foreign land at government expense, following which they would contract to spend one or two years as an escort-interpreter. This possibility might be explored on a modest experimental basis before any major step is taken. In addition to providing capable escort-interpreters, the expense to the government might be justified because this approach could provide potential Foreign Service officer material or permanent employees in the Division of Language Services. A few Fulbright scholars returning from overseas might be willing to serve as escort-interpreters. Over a period of time, individuals who have had experience overseas in the new Peace Corps may become another resource.

Any heavier use of foreign graduate students attending American universities seems inadvisable in view of the relative inadequacy of their background regarding the American scene. Nonetheless, some guarded use of this resource appears both necessary and feasible. In order to prevent flagrant failures by escort-interpreters, it may be necessary that a more careful check be made before a leader requiring an escort-interpreter is allowed to depart for America so that an adequate aide can be provided. A postponement or no trip at all may be better than sixty days with an unsatisfactory escort-interpreter.

A higher percentage of the contract interpreters could be made effective if the Division of Language Services were given funds to conduct a training program for escort-interpreters. The present informal orientation is not enough. At least a one-month course given to the most promising of the contract interpreters, possibly including orientation at the Washington International Center or the Foreign Service Institute, might yield substantial results and overcome many of the current difficulties. Careful supervision of these trainees over a month would help appraise capabilities and provide a better basis for selection.

In the case of those individuals programmed by the Department of State directly, it is suggested that in appropriate instances an advance escort might precede the visitor and the escort by several days to work out with local program officers a firm schedule of events. The advance escort—who would not have to speak a foreign language—would maintain liaison with the leader and his accompanying escort as well as the programming office in the Department of State. Use of an experienced individual in the advance role would enable the leader's program to be adapted to his needs en route, and the local program officer would be less diverted from the programming of typical foreign leaders. One of the problems at present is the relative neglect of many typical leaders because of the need to give extra attention to the few. In trying to please the few there is a failure to please the more typical leader. While an advance escort policy would seem expensive, judiciously used, it might pay for itself many times.

At the conclusion of a trip, a report on the tour is prepared by the escort-interpreter for the Division of Language Services. Such reports are forwarded to the contract agencies when special program problems have arisen and there is criticism of the agencies. Otherwise, the agencies rely for evaluation of their programming mostly upon two informal discussions—both usually brief and sketchy—one between the escort-interpreter and the appropriate program officer, and the other with the departing leader.

This discussion of problems should not be allowed to obscure the fact that much good work is being done by escort and interpreter personnel. Possibly the most satisfying discovery during the entire survey of the program was the abundant evidence of sensitivity on the part of the permanent personnel in the Division of Language Services regarding the problems of cross-cultural communication. At the same time, as the above comments suggest, there is room for substantial improvement.

5

Community Participation

IT IS IN THE CITIES AND TOWNS—whether on Main Street, in apartments or offices, churches, ball parks, museums, or industrial establishments—and in suburban homes and on farms, that the foreign leader confronts American reality. The vital heart of the Foreign Leader Program and the key to its relative effectiveness must lie in the personal contacts and experiences arranged by local sponsors or occurring spontaneously. The continuance and growth of governmental exchange programs place an increasing burden on citizens in local communities across America. This fact must be acknowledged, and the federal government must accept its share of responsibility and help to resolve a variety of emerging problems. The Department of State must find means of cooperating with local groups to provide an operational framework adequate to meet the essential needs of the present and to grow in response to the greater challenge of tomorrow.

There are seven general categories of local sponsors. *First*, there are the Department of State reception centers, staffed by Foreign Service and civil service personnel and generally functioning in cities heavily used by the leader and specialist programs. *Second*, there are the two "contract" centers of the Institute of International Education, staffed by paid nongovernmental personnel and a few volunteers, which service other urban areas deeply involved in the leader and specialist programs. *Third*, there are local sponsoring organizations which raise their own funds and have been established especially to handle foreign visitors; these have small paid staffs and rely primarily on volunteers. Nonetheless, they handle a considerable volume of leaders and specialists. A *fourth* type, somewhat similarly staffed and financed and bearing a similar workload, operates as part of an already functioning voluntary organization whose primary interest is foreign relations, for example, Councils on World Affairs. A *fifth* type, usually but not necessarily functioning in a smaller city, can be distinguished from the previous category because it functions as an adjunct of a voluntary organization with interests other than foreign affairs, perhaps a university or a chamber of commerce. A *sixth* type handles only labor leaders and devotes itself primarily to organizing substantive discussions on labor problems. This type is the adjunct of a labor organization and normally functions in large cities. It tends to depend for hospitality and sightseeing upon another local program sponsor in the same city. The *seventh* type is the lone individual, usually found in a small town, who single-handedly with the cooperation of his friends and neighbors programs several leaders per year, taking time from his business or profession and money from his own pocket to make the visits as useful as possible.

In a number of large cities, two of these categories may be functioning at the same time, each handling a separate aspect of the leaders' programs. The usual division of operations is between substantive activities and home hospitality or sightseeing. Sometimes the several sponsors in a given city have blended and coordinated their efforts rather successfully. In other instances, a struggle for leadership is in progress, behind the scenes and in the open, with little cooperation and only fitful coordination.

In many medium-sized to large cities, the local sponsors handle all types of foreign visitors, those coming by private programs as well as those brought by a variety of governmental programs. In others, the organization deals with only leaders and specialists. In no instance does an organization exist for leaders alone, although the one-man sponsor in a small town may deal mostly with leaders. This diversity of programming arrangements, coupled with the varied objectives of the leaders themselves, sometimes makes local leader programs indistinguishable from those of other foreign visitors. The leader's lack of status symbols and his unpredictable interests have made it difficult for program officers of the local sponsors to remain aware of "leaders" as a category separate from "foreign visitors" in general or from "specialists" in particular, or to meet adequately any distinctive purposes of the Foreign Leader Program.

PROGRAMMING PROBLEMS

Before discussing the most apparent problems in local programming—of which there are many—it is well to emphasize that there is much to praise. Many leaders find satisfying and enlightening experiences in most of the communities they visit. Program officers work sincerely, often with dedication, to further the interests of the enterprise. Instances of personal sacrifice of time and money abound. In a job which is often underpaid or which is a voluntary service on top of family and other commitments, several thousand Americans are doing their utmost to make the program a success. On balance, the results of their efforts have been good, but it is probable that, with more support and with improvements in the approach, much more could be accomplished.

Though problems vary from city to city, there appear to be some basic recurring difficulties—pressure points which indicate the need to change emphases or to move in new directions. These problems are recognized by many people in the Department of State, the contract agencies, and the local communities.

One difficulty is that there is a tendency to schedule too many discussions with a leader's American counterparts. When he arrives at the contract agency, he often seems more interested in pursuing some special topic relevant to his own professional field than anything else. As a result, much of his program is designed to achieve this end. By mid-trip, however, the typical leader's enthusiasm has waned. The few dedicated souls who never tire are in the minority.

Related to the excessive scheduling of counterparts is the heavy concentration on viewing physical plants, whether it be schools, hospitals, city halls, or museums. By the time a typical journalistic leader has tramped through press rooms across America, observing everything from the simple small town press to the complex machinery of the giants, he is not enthusiastic about seeing another one. The editors are not interested in talking with visiting newsmen in such great numbers because of the time involved and the lack of any personal gain from the conversations. So the leaders are passed on to some lower-ranking functionary for a tour of the plant.

Another sore point in the counterpart emphasis involves the area studies institutes on university campuses. In the past, the Department of State assumed that the area experts would want to talk with all visiting leaders from their areas, that there would be significant mutual benefit from these exchanges. By now, many of the experts are indifferent to the whole program. They feel that the visits are so short and the leaders so poorly matched to their own interests that chitchat is all that is feasible. Most of the American experts have developed better sources of information, and they are not particularly interested in conveying a broad understanding of the American scene. Overuse has seriously eroded their original enthusiasm.

Insufficient attention is devoted in most cities to the exploration and cultivation of new program resources. Operations move at such a rapid pace during most of the year that it is easier to schedule something that the program officer is already familiar with than to open up new contacts. As a result, new resources sometimes wither through disuse while old resources disintegrate from overuse. Some of the overload on the few stems from poor orientation overseas or in the contract agencies which often directs the leader to the best known and most overused individuals. The busy expert may be a less useful contact in some cases than some relatively unknown generalist. The problem is for the program officer to know his community well enough so that he can get beyond the celebrity to the less publicized citizen.

As a result of finding many foreign leaders tired of counterparts or "mechanisms", the program officers involved from the midpoint of a leader's trip onward have found it difficult to do much advance planning. Too often the leader is not interested in doing what has been arranged for him. This has meant pressure upon the leader to persuade him to comply with plans already made so that program resources will not be offended into premature retirement. In not a few instances, the leader arrives so fatigued that he wants to do nothing but rest in blissful isolation. So it has been realistic for program officers to make only the most tentative plans before the leader's arrival. In many instances this has meant that the leader's time has been wasted on sightseeing which did not interest him or on routine contacts which could be quickly arranged while the things he really wanted to do could be worked out. Sometimes the persons who could best meet the program need have been absent from the city, although they might have rearranged their schedules had they known ahead of time that their presence would be useful.

Sometimes a visiting leader wants to lecture on his native land or his speciality in the course of his tour. It is occasionally a problem for local program officers to furnish him with a proper audience, one that will be interested in the leader as a person and what he has to say. There are those who question whether the leader learns about America by talking about his own land and personal interests. It seems more likely, however, that the exchange between a leader and an interested audience does strengthen his understanding of the United States and its people. It may also stimulate American interest in the leader and his country and make the rest of the visit in the community more productive. Public exchanges may pose public relations problems, of course, so program officers must schedule public appearances with caution. Because of the problems involved, including occasional doubt about the visitor's ability to speak English clearly, fewer speaking engagements are arranged than might be desirable.

The program officer finds some difficulty in persuading many individuals to cooperate in the substantive elements of a leader's interview program. Why should an advertising specialist spend time with a visiting educator; a newspaper editor, with a philosopher; an economist, with a museum director? This is particularly difficult to justify when these same men will be talking with visitors under the Specialists Program in which there is more emphasis on communication between experts in the same field. As a result, those who tend to cooperate are those with personal interests, of a political, economic, or social nature, to serve. What they offer may be calculated primarily to effect their personal advancement, not to give the foreign leader a full and fair view of the American scene.

Industrial concerns have been somewhat reluctant to cooperate with the Leader Program because they have seen little advantage in it for themselves. Few of the leaders are industrialists. Even when they are, American industry is sometimes reluctant to take visitors through its plants for fear that ideas will be appropriated to benefit foreign competitors. Unless a concern is interested in the leader's country and the leader plays a role related to this end, many industrial organizations consider foreign visitors a distraction which they would rather avoid. As a result, program officers often send leaders to visit the "old reliables" whether they are appropriate or not.

If there is a general underemphasis on American industry, there is an overemphasis on trade unions in the labor part of the program. The programs of visiting labor leaders, worked out through the Trade Union Division of the Office of International Labor Affairs, Department of Labor, schedule counterpart-to-counterpart contacts almost to the exclusion of a broader view of the United States. Nor do labor leaders generally get a good cross section of American hospitality. Because the labor leader is handled for substantive programming by labor unions instead of by the normal channels for other types of visitors, the local sponsors who are non-labor are sometimes less interested in arranging sightseeing, home hospitality, or visits to cultural events for labor leaders than for other leaders. As a result, many labor leaders have fewer opportunities than other visitors to be entertained in American homes—unless it be an occasional labor home.

Few of the foreign visitors have any real opportunity to pursue secondary contacts they may establish as they move through the program arranged by the local sponsor. Because of the swift pace of the visits and the brevity of time in each city, the opportunity to build on the chance meeting—the happy accident—which brings together a leader and someone with whom he finds a sympathetic bond is minimized.

While it is probably impossible not to depend primarily upon hotels for accommodations—and most of the time the leaders may prefer them—it must be remembered that, if the visitor remains at the hotel and is dependent upon his own efforts for evening entertainment throughout most of his visit, his view of the American scene is likely to be distorted. Middle-class American hotels have a sameness that is deadening. And the type of evening diversion open to the casual visitor is unimpressive. While this is part of the truth about America, it is only a small part and not a very creditable part. If there is café society, it contributes little to understanding the American scene unless it is kept in perspective. It is regrettable, therefore, that the typical leader spends so much of his time in public accommodations, missing many opportunities for more intimate experiences in American homes as well as cultural and civic events of greater import to the basic purposes for which he has come.

The rate of flow is also important. There are times during the year when few foreign visitors pass through American cities, when each visiting leader can receive considerable individual attention, when new contacts can be opened up and old standbys need not be overworked. There are other times when fifteen leaders may be waiting to talk with one of three program officers. A quiet atmosphere, without a distracting line of waiting leaders, makes possible greater understanding and sympathy between leader and officer. Even if volunteers can be brought in at overload times, they are less likely to do as effective programming as the regular officers and are likely to find themselves working in crowded and unpleasant surroundings.

Although some local sponsors provide spacious reception quarters, the staff customarily works in an unpartitioned noisy room which hampers efficiency. If a few offices are tastefully furnished, others are undistinguished. Foreign leaders are always met at their hotels in one particular city, often included in the circuit, because the headquarters of the group taking care of foreign visitors in the city is on the second floor of a rather uninviting temporary building. Although the university in the city is the principal attraction for some one-third of the visitors who go there, the university charges rent for the inadequate space it has made available and makes no direct financial contribution for the support of the voluntary organization programming the visitors. In several of the larger cities, the centers seem to have been selected as hide-aways rather than as locations easily and conveniently found.

The saving grace is the general pleasantness of staff members once the office is located. If there is one thing which stands out as the unknown visitor walks through the door—at least during a quiet period—it is the friendly greeting of some member of the staff long before the visitor and his interest are identified. Whether this same feeling can be conveyed in more trying times of the year is open to question, but the spirit appears willing and many of the personnel dedicated. Beneath the happy exterior, however, there are tensions. Salaries are exceptionally low, particularly outside of the Department of State reception centers. One of the major noncontract centers is directed by an individual—obviously of considerable talent and energy—who is paid approximately $4,800 annually. Some have criticized the youth and inexperience of program officers in one of the major contract centers, but the top salary that can be paid for such services in that organization is under $5,000 per year. Turnover in the programming posts is high. Most incumbents are working for graduate degrees and waiting for the day when they can move on. It is unfortunate that the few Department of State contracts now in operation should be so stringent that they impose serious personnel problems.

Men can hardly afford to be involved on a full-time basis if they have families, even where salaries are paid. Among men, it is the elderly or partially disabled or those with some private income who can serve as volunteers. Among women, it is those of the upper-middle class who have come forward to meet the need. These women are able and energetic, but their minds are on many things. The work is not viewed as a permanent profession, even though they may over a period of time have gained many useful insights into cross-cultural relations. In middle-sized cities, the programming is often done as one small phase of a larger job, as a sideline from which no promotion can be expected and for which no compensation is received. In the small community, the one-man sponsor makes a real sacrifice of time, effort, and money for the duration of a leader's visit.

The funds available for the budgets of the local program sponsors are severely limited. The Department of State reception centers are better off than most of the other organizations so far as office space and salaries are concerned. But the centers are anything but impressive. They are often staffed at too low a rank and have only meager funds for entertainment. Every dinner must be wheedled out of some interested or long-suffering individual. To limit a Department of State center to less than twenty-five cents per visitor for entertainment is extreme parsimony. Low salaries normally result in a fearful avoidance of any situation which might call for personal expenditures.

The "contract" local sponsors are less adequately financed than the reception centers. Some staff members believe that the Department of State sometimes comes forward with complaints about the programming at the time the contract is being renegotiated in order to counter requests for additional funds. Salaries are extremely low and the personnel, though carefully chosen, are no more than barely adequate.

Local sponsors attached to general foreign affairs organizations are in a peculiarly difficult financial situation. Such an organization finds it difficult to increase its fundraising to meet its requirements for the Leader Program. New sources of funds, which might give to an action program of the leader type, may be reluctant to contribute to a general educational organization. Because of their limited financial resources, some consider general educational organizations ill-adapted to the needs of the Leader Program.

Voluntary groups which have come into being especially to service foreign visitors have also had their fundraising problems. Few can afford even one paid staff member. Many have inadequate physical facilities. A major factor determining the leadership of many such organizations appears to be the amount of money contributed to the entertainment of foreign visitors. The budgets barely cover office space and materials, possibly an ill-paid secretary with part-time student assistants. From here on, the well to do take over and spend from their personal funds as necessary to keep the program going. This would seem to be a jerry-built system, hardly sufficient for a well-organized performance. This is not to say that these people are not doing a good job considering the trying circumstances. But how long can the operation continue in this fashion? Has attrition not already set in? Even in a small one-man-sponsor town, a leading citizen suggested the need for funds to be used when the one-man sponsor is busy and cannot drive to meet the visitor arriving in a larger city twenty miles away. An underpaid secretary, serving a voluntary organization, asked if the government did not have some obligation to pay a minimum "head tax" per visitor programmed through her city.

There is no doubt that some very hard-working people are carrying the unglamorous administrative load of the Foreign Leader Program on salaries so low that it is inconceivable that competent personnel will long remain under such conditions. There will always be those seeking the thrill of entertaining the foreign visitor or those with an interest in doing something for the program, but there is little glamor in performing the continuing everyday tasks. And the dedicated are not always able. Yet the proper performance of the local sponsor function is necessary to the success of the program. If volunteers would give their full time for a prolonged period to such tasks, it would be a major contribution. The fact that they can usually be present on only an intermittent basis, a day or so a week, limits their usefulness. Rapid turnover and "on-again, off-again" activity hardly contribute to administrative efficiency.

Turnover among poorly paid full-time employees, and attrition among volunteers, most of whom bring little background in crosscultural relations to their posts, suggest the need for an active inservice training program, at least in the larger cities with a heavy flow of foreign visitors. At present, there is little such training. An able head of a local agency can teach much in staff conferences when there is time. Special programs can be held from time to time for volunteers, usually in the evening. But the leadership is not always so gifted, and training given to volunteers must be so diluted by "tea and cookies" to stimulate interest that forward motion educationally may not be worth the effort. There are able volunteers who have served for prolonged periods of time, but such persons are rare.

The typical local sponsor appears to be functioning in a hectic "catch as catch can" fashion with the hope, but hardly the certainty, of always coming down on his feet. There has been little time to get in touch with other program sponsors to discuss common problems. The Department of State and the contract agencies have recently exercised leadership in starting this type of exchange. The organization of regular communication among the local sponsors and the creation of the National Council for Community Services to International Visitors, a central clearinghouse, are long overdue steps in the right direction. Such actions will be of only limited value, however, without stronger financial resources for the local communities. The exchange of ideas may stimulate more effective programming, fundraising and staffing, but realization of the fruits of these steps is a slow process. On the basis of past experience, this appears to be a "bootstrap" operation in quicksand.

One aspect of the problem is the use of public relations as a means of improving the financial situation of the local sponsors. Some already appear to be well organized and to be receiving professional assistance in furthering their development. Public relations can help not only in raising funds and expanding host resources but also in satisfying the status needs of the visiting leaders through contacts with the mass media and with local organizations in need of speakers.

Such activities, however, may be an unreliable tool in the hands of the untrained or the unwary. Public relations require skill, time, and personnel, plus a sense of purpose. Most of the local sponsors have been unable to mobilize these prerequisites adequately. The right professional consultant may not always be available on a voluntary basis, and for most sponsors it is visionary to anticipate such services on a paid basis.

ALTERNATE EMPHASES IN ORGANIZATION OF LOCAL SPONSORS

Several critical questions suggest themselves. The most significant is: *Should the present diversity of local sponsors be continued?* Local sponsors may now be an office of the Department of State, or a contract organization, an unpaid private organization, or an individual citizen. Some have suggested that the Department of State set up offices in every city where foreign visitors would be programmed. One suggestion made more than ten years ago called for 175 such offices scattered about America. This would have involved services not only to foreign leaders but to other foreign visitors as well. A recommendation for the establishment of five additional Department of State reception centers is considered more realistic today by several program administrators. Others connected with the Leader Program believe that contracts should be made with organizations in additional cities, Denver and Chicago being the only two centers functioning under such an arrangement at the present time. Certain groups outside government suggest that all programming in local communities be turned over to individual private citizens, each of whom would take a visiting leader into his home to participate in family and community life for a time—the host perhaps traveling with the individual to regional points of interest— and then pass him on to another such individual.

Should the Department of State establish a large number of additional governmental centers? The arguments for such a move start from the premise that "if you want a thing done well, do it yourself." Creation of such a chain of governmental offices would make the administrative hierarchy much neater. It would make clear to the foreign leader that at all times he would be assisted directly by the Department of State. Given the prestige of the Department, requests for leader interviews with local citizens might evoke a better response than a request from a nongovernmental staff. Communication among the programming centers would probably be improved.

The establishment of such a system of centers would involve a greatly increased budget. The ideal of furthering local community activity through private citizens might be disparaged. With current staffing patterns, which would require one or more Foreign Service officers in each center, the matter of meeting the personnel requirements would be a serious problem. Under close departmental supervision, the foreign leaders might feel they were not getting a full and fair view of America. If local citizens were hired as civil service employees, there would be the problem of maintaining adequate relationships between the field and headquarters. Long periods of service in a single field post are not conducive to a comprehensive understanding of the broader aspects of the program.

A case can be made for the establishment of five additional Department of State reception centers at strategic geographic locations of relatively heavy use in the Leader Program. It can hardly be argued that such centers would necessarily be able to provide any better programming than could be done by contract agencies operating under less stringent agreements than those presently in effect with the Department of State. But, if the present reception centers and those being considered here could be organized to perform a field office function for the Leaders and Specialists Division, they might be quite useful.

Such regional offices could be used to help communities organize themselves to participate in the Leader and Specialists Programs. Center personnel could be available for individual consultation or to organize regional conferences of local sponsors. Leaders handled directly by the Department would often be programmed by these reception centers, and their personnel would be able to provide guidance to such visitors and their escort-interpreters at reasonable intervals throughout their tours. Regular reporting on programming problems by the new offices might enable the Department to take remedial action more promptly.

On the other hand, there is much to be said for leaving programming in the hands of present local sponsors and establishing small regional field offices at strategic locations if the Department feels a need for more positive regional action and supervision. The handling of the programming function during peak-load periods might prevent adequate performance of the leadership and supervisory functions by reception centers performing multiple functions.

There has been a call for increasing the number of private organizations under contract with the Government. In view of several unfortunate experiences, there are some who would reject this suggestion without further consideration. Such contract sponsors have not always been able to provide sufficient salaries to attract and hold adequate program officers who could make a long-time profession of cross-cultural relations. Use of such private organizations means less governmental control than if government centers were relied upon. The fact that contracts are renewed annually, however, gives the Department of State considerable control. The local centers can draw for leadership upon persons of stature in the local community. The contract relationship allows such organizations to use the prestige of the Department in behalf of the program. Such leadership can rely upon its own contacts to stimulate private initiative in behalf of the program.

Use of respected institutions as contract organizations can remove the "guided tour" stigma from local programming without dependence upon temporary volunteers. There is a need for stable, well-paid staffs. It seems unlikely that these can be provided without some form of governmental assistance. There is a need for representation allowances so that professional staff members can play a more important role in dealing with leaders and not have to rely so much on certain private citizens simply because they have the funds to entertain foreign visitors. With larger and better-paid staffs, local program officers could play an orientation role which would make the leaders' visits more meaningful. Much can be said, therefore, in favor of the use of contract organizations in a few additional cities with heavy leader workloads. To be successful, such an expansion would require realistic contracts of a less austere nature than those now in effect.

Some argue that continued use of unpaid local voluntary organizations has merit. They say that the need to seek funds keeps initiative at the local level, that the absence of governmental support lets the visitor know that he is seeing America with "no strings attached." So long as workloads are not too heavy, volunteers can do most of the work. All that may be required in the way of paid personnel is a secretary.

Continued reliance, however, upon spasmodic participation by volunteer personnel, without strong continuing leadership and planning, seems unwise. Citizens in some cities have been able to raise funds to hire a permanent professional leader to handle over-all programming responsibility and to supervise volunteers. This is a step forward, but it may not be enough. Funds available have not been sufficient to pay the salaries necessary to make such leadership effective. It is doubtful that volunteers can program adequately when they serve on an intermittent basis. Such tasks as building program resources require constant attention and few conflicting interests. Follow-through to assess contacts used is important. Volunteers can do this but are likely not to do as well as permanent paid personnel. In most instances, volunteers might be better utilized as members of advisory committees for special projects rather than in day-to-day programming or administrative duties.

It would appear that some device for providing governmental funds to supplement local funds is necessary, even in a number of cities now trying to go it alone. Of course, some of the load on these cities may be lessened as attempts are made to program leaders into a wider variety of cities. Even so, volunteers have limited utility. If the contract causes citizens to give up private fundraising to cover basic costs, local initiative can be preserved by private financing of special activities which may have more appeal than support for general administration. In smaller cities, where the number of visitors is not sufficient to make administration of the leader program a full-time job, some formula of assistance based on payment to cover basic administrative costs for each visitor might be worked out. If anyone thinks that these types of government assistance will take away the opportunity of Americans to contribute to the Leader Program, he is mistaken. No one suggests that the many resource people who meet with the foreign leaders should be paid except in the most unusual circumstances. Modest governmental assistance to provide an adequate local coordinating office can make the effort expended by other individuals in the community far more effective.

Some persons with a strong feeling for individual-to-individual exchanges have advocated separation of the Foreign Leader Program from the kind of local sponsors now functioning in medium-sized and larger cities. Under such a plan, a private individual might be given a vacation by his employer for a two-week period now and then to take over the entertainment and programming of a visiting foreign leader. The leader would live in the home of the man responsible for his visit, thus having an opportunity to observe an American home directly and continuously. The host might accompany the leader on side tours to persons or points of interest in his region before transferring the visitor to another host in another community. This plan increases the personal contact of the visitor with American home life and enables him always to be accompanied by someone who is thoroughly familiar with the local situation.

These assets are more than offset by heavy disadvantages. The basic assumption of this suggestion is that most Americans thoroughly understand their own communities and could provide a visitor with a balanced and sophisticated interpretation of them. It assumes that a rather wide variety of Americans could be freed from their regular obligations to participate in such a program. It assumes that such individuals are capable of successful cross-cultural relationships for extended periods of time. These assumptions can be seriously questioned.

What happens when the relations of leader and host become strained during such a visit, as they will on some occasions? Will the personnel available represent a good political, economic, and social cross-section of American society? Would those who could not afford to take so active a part be willing to trust their more affluent fellow Americans to give the visitor a balanced view of the American scene? What supervision would such individuals accept from a contract agency or from the Department of State? What type of program reporting would they be willing to perform? How objective would it be? How would such volunteers be selected or trained? Might not the turnover of individuals participating be relatively large so that the experience would be lost almost as soon as it had been gained? This proposal opens a Pandora's box of new problems. It rejects the known for the unknown before sufficient effort has been made to make the known work better.

An analysis of the foregoing arguments leads to the conclusion that the number of Department of State centers need not necessarily be expanded immediately, that the creation of small regional field offices by the Department would be useful, and that additional monetary assistance to local communities is a necessity. In a number of instances, particularly in the largest cities, it would seem necessary for contracts to cover all expenses of programming and reporting of leader visits. In somewhat less heavily used cities, where private organizations are now struggling valiantly to raise funds with only modest success, contracts might provide for basic administrative costs essential to the provision of central leadership and stable staffing. Private initiative would be encouraged through emphasis on advisory groups and the meeting of special needs through local fund projects.

The approach relying upon sustained use of individual hosts is rejected because its advantages can be realized and its disadvantages overcome within the present framework if the adjustments just suggested are incorporated in the program. A major problem in programming leaders to small towns is finding in each such community a key individual who not only is part of the American scene but understands it. The creation of small regional offices under the Leaders and Specialists Division would assist in this task.

An important subsidiary question which is related to the type of local program sponsor but which deals with only the programming of labor leaders is: *Should labor leaders continue to be programmed separately from all other foreign leaders?* At the outset, it should be realized that the Department of Labor is already attempting to broaden the local programming of labor leaders. It may be that some labor leaders would be uneasy if programmed by present local sponsors in view of the upper-middle-class orientation of many volunteers. Quite likely the resources presently possessed by the local sponsors would not be adequate to meet the needs of visiting labor leaders. However, when more skilled central staffs can be established, transfer of the programming of labor leaders from labor unions to the central local sponsor would become more feasible and probably advisable. Timing such a shift would have to be made on a city-by-city basis. In some cities the program load of the central local sponsors would be heavy enough to make an additional burden difficult to assume rapidly. While any change is likely to be resisted, it may be brought about successfully if the labor unions are assured that their interests are not to be ignored and that the central local sponsors, backed by governmental funds and with professional programming officers, will no longer be unrepresentative of the broad range of American interest groups.

GENERAL CONCLUSIONS

The over-all purpose of local programming is to develop in the typical visiting leader some comprehension of the true nature of various segments of American society: how they function internally and in relation to other communities and levels of government, their family life, civic and cultural activities. The challenge to the Leader Program is to allow the average grantee to understand the complexity of the community in action and to see the relationship of each of its major parts to the whole. Problems of American society need not and should not be hidden. Nor does their discussion need to be accompanied by wailing and beating of breasts. They must be viewed in the total context. Only by carefully developing such a comprehensive view, with exploratory ventures into more detailed aspects, can the foreign leader gain any insight into American behavior. Present programming tends to present local experiences as discrete and unrelated parts. There is some variety of observation but little integration, and too much of the ceremony is not directly relevant to basic program purposes. The average leader moves on before he understands how the observations he has made fit into the over-all community process.

Too often the leader's view—achieved mostly through his counterparts' eyes—may be just as distorted as was the original image which he brought from his homeland. The leader sometimes remains outside the real community during his visit, transient and anonymous, without being drawn into a warm circle of interest and friendship. Further development of resources for both substantive discussion and various forms of hospitality is badly needed in many cities. The role of the local program officers and well chosen resources in assisting the foreign leader to integrate his experiences into a comprehensible whole before he moves on to another community needs to be strengthened. With even the best orientation, programming, and guidance, the leader is likely to suffer some mental indigestion as he tries to achieve the full and fair view of the American scene in sixty days. With better local resources, this indigestion should be less acute than it has been in the past. If communities should improve programming of a general nature, they should also improve their abilities to provide tailor-made experiences for special purpose visitors who might be programmed directly by the Department of State. To do all of this, local sponsors need stronger outside guidance and financial assistance.

6

Terminal Procedures

THE END OF THE STUDY TOUR is only the beginning of understanding American life. "The American people remain a mystery. They are too numerous and too restless," James Reston has aptly said in the *New York Times,* commenting on the difficulties of prognosticating the results of American national elections. If American experts are confused, how much more difficult it is for typical "60-day wonders" of the Foreign Leader Program to grasp the American mood. Both, Reston might say, "are trying to put calipers on a continent that won't stand still, that is restless in mind and body."

There has been a tendency on the part of the Department of State to be rather pleased when foreign leaders end their tours in a sort of happy daze, even though it is well aware that this state of mind may wear off over a period of time. Through the years there has been an almost desperate search for favorable comments from returned leaders about "the American way," even though there was no shortage of them. This was, in part, a response to the necessities of Executive Branch dependence upon congressional appropriations. The Department has wondered and worried when leaders left America with a strongly unfavorable impression. One can guess that the most useful suggestions for improvement of program operations and the best basis for the development of further cross-cultural understanding have been the reflections of leaders who have been able to make balanced judgments of their experience under the program.

In current circumstances, few leaders are in any position to make a careful assessment of either procedures or substance as they race through exit interviews and head for home. At that stage, they are trying to be gracious visitors expressing thanks for the tour, or they are disgruntled and ready to argue with each American administrator they meet. Even those who fall somewhere in between are not likely to have digested the experience fully. Yet, there is much to be said for recording their spontaneous reactions, recognizing the limitations and the danger of relying upon them alone. The Department of State has not been unaware of this problem and has sought later evaluations from the field. It often takes several months or a year for the experience to crystallize in a returned leader's mind. Only slowly does he become aware of any fundamental changes in his way of thinking about the United States and its people.

TERMINAL SEMINARS

Few leaders have been fortunate enough in the past to participate in terminal seminars on the general significance of their experience. Most have gone home after the "quick look" at America without even a "quick think" about what they have seen. There should be built into the program an opportunity for an organized discussion of the most important aspects of American life in relation to other societies after the leader has had his chance to see the country and talk with its people.

There are several purposes that such seminars might serve, but knowledge is lacking concerning whether a single seminar experience can satisfactorily serve multiple purposes. Indeed, sufficient knowledge is lacking to determine which among several possible purposes deserve priority, or on what basis priorities might be varied to suit different groups of grantees. There exists some feeling that the purpose of the seminar should be to help bring the observations of the visitor into clearer focus, without any attempt to underestimate (or overestimate) American problems or to oversell (or undersell) American virtues. The agenda to achieve such a purpose might include problems common to the nations of all participants so that attention could be given to resolving common difficulties rather than allowing primary concentration on American shortcomings. Among competing purposes to be achieved in a seminar might be: (1) a further explanation of American life after the visitor has considerable background for understanding what is said; (2) the evaluation of changes in the individual visitor's thinking as a result of the visit; or (3) just an opportunity for the visitor to get some things off his chest that he has not had a chance to express during the trip. All of these purposes may be served during a total seminar experience, but it is possible that an emphasis put upon some of these purposes will limit the degree to which others can be furthered.

No one who has observed a terminal seminar can be unaware of the many difficulties posed by such a conference. The leader participants come with some doubts regarding who is sponsoring the discussion and how objective the exchange is to be. Some are in a hurry to get home; others are fatigued. For many, the jumble of what they have observed remains unorganized and relatively meaningless. It is difficult to bring together a group with sufficient common background to serve as a basis of successful communication. Language differences necessitate the use of interpreters which can slow discussion to a snail's pace and bore some beyond endurance. Then there are the problems of finding able and vigorous American participants and a suitable site, somewhat removed from the distractions of a major urban center.

Past experience suggests that the terminal seminar should be run under the leadership of an academic institution with a reputation for objective scholarship. To do less is to invite doubts about the value of the effort. In view of the effects of fatigue and the desire to begin preparations for the trip home, it would seem wise to make the seminar a residence experience in order to concentrate attention. Sufficient time should be allowed for arranging the formalities of departure—with a day or so of free time provided in the port of departure—and the leader should be informed that he will not be under pressure as he leaves.

If all departing leaders were urged, and for all practical purposes required, to participate in a terminal seminar, the numbers involved would be sufficient during many months of the year to group participants in ways that would ensure some common bases for discussion. It would be necessary to provide a staff that would make the experience satisfying. This would probably require the use of resident discussion leaders supplemented by visiting experts who would be given expenses and adequate honoraria for their services. The location would need to be near an ample source of talent so that outstanding men could participate without being exhausted by overparticipation. Insofar as possible, simultaneous translation of the discussions at the seminars is to be preferred, but this poses logistic problems which are not easily met.

Seminars, more or less experimental in nature, have been held at the University of Pittsburgh and at Tregaron—the estate of former Ambassador Joseph Davies in Washington, D.C.—among other places. The facilities of neither center provide a residence experience. Program officers have found Pittsburgh a bit remote to work into schedules with regularity, and the Pittsburgh seminars have been run on a fixed schedule that is not always convenient. Tregaron, without residence facilities, has found it difficult to hold participants during their last few days as they prepare to depart.

The seminar should probably be no less than three days in length, with formal discussion during the day being supplemented by recreational opportunities and informal discussions in the late afternoon and evening. It takes time for the participants to relax and become part of the group. On the other hand, to hold the leaders longer would be unwise. It is better to end the discussions while there is still life in them than to continue until all the questions and participants have been exhausted. In view of the general circumstances in which the seminars are held, they should perhaps be viewed more as an opportunity for leaders to begin thinking about common problems which exist for America and their own lands rather than as a device to provide definitive answers. Like all good educational experiences, the terminal seminar should be more a beginning than an ending.

EVALUATION BEFORE DEPARTURE

Evaluation of a tour is provided first of all in the program reports by escort-interpreters prepared relatively quickly at the close of a trip. One has the impression that these reports, when done by able men, are the most valuable evidence immediately available on the leader's feelings about his programming. But not all leaders are accompanied during their tours. The Department of State reception centers and the contract local program sponsors also file reports and sometimes telephone comments on the results of a visit in a particular city. Often these are not made in time for their contents to be useful in improving the programs reported, but they are available for subsequent analysis as an indication of the leaders' feelings en route and as a basis of doing a better job on other trips.

Upon his return to Washington, the foreign leader talks first with his program officer in the contract agency and then with the area officer in the Leaders Branch of the Leaders and Specialists Division, Department of State. Neither of these exit interviews is functioning adequately at the present time. Leaders sometimes have to be coaxed to visit the contract agencies upon their return to Washington. When the leaders do come in, either with or without an invitation, most of the discussions produce little information useful for program evaluation. As a result, reports of exit interviews in the contract agencies tend to be routine; some officers may not even take the trouble to write up their notes until a year later. Reports on problem cases may be forwarded to the Department more rapidly. So far as exit interviews in the Department are concerned, quite often they are not held at all. Even when they are held, reports are not always filed. Here is an overburdened administrative machine eliminating functions that are not a part of daily operations but that might be useful in program evaluation. This response, though natural, is contributory to the present difficulty in maintaining a continuing appraisal of the program.

Typical questions in the two exit interviews include the following: "Is there anything you expected to find in this country that you did not find?" "Is there anything you did not expect to find that you did find?" "Did you do everything you wanted to do?" "Was there anything about the trip that was outstanding?" "What do you remember most, either good or bad, about the trip?" "If you had it to do over again, what would you change?" Discussions tend to take off from these questions into the realm of the visitor's specialized field of interest or into points concerning experiences in individual cities.

If the interviewing officer is well briefed on the visitor's past views, he is in a position to probe gently for evidence of change or reaction to experiences planned to correct what had appeared to be distortions in the visitor's thinking. Such biographic information, it should be recalled, has not always been made available in sufficient detail to either the program officer in the contract agency or the area officer in the Department. The usefulness of the interview may depend upon the degree of pressure under which the interviewer is working or the pace of the visitor's trip and his degree of fatigue. Certainly the results are heavily colored by the visitor's cultural background. It is almost impossible to get some visitors to speak freely and analytically even under the best of circumstances. One has the feeling that all parties concerned tend to exude a hearty spirit of good fellowship, but that often interviewer and leader think of the interview as a mere formality and are in a hurry to get on to something else.

Considering means of increasing the effectiveness and usefulness of the exit interview, three conclusions come to mind. A more reflective program, with a terminal seminar in the period just before the interview, would be likely to place the foreign leader in a better frame of mind for the discussion. As staffing becomes less stringent and as program loads are somewhat stabilized in the contract agencies, program officers would have more time to give to both interviews and writing reports. As area officers in the Leaders Branch get rid of more administrative detail, possibly they will become more interested in exit interviews and the preparation of reports.

There are some real drawbacks, however, to following this course. It seems doubtful if "operators" will ever become really interested in evaluation. The changes that would make greater interest possible seem likely to take place rather slowly, with the time gained probably spread over improving a number of aspects of the Leader Program. Thus the released time and energy will not all be directed toward improving the exit interviews and reporting. Another matter of concern is that the foreign leader must take part in two exit interviews, one at the contract agency and another at the Department of State. Saying farewell is almost as painful a process as the delicate matter of being oriented.

It may be that the real exit interview responsibility could be assumed by the new Department of State reception center in Washington, if it were to be adequately staffed for interviewing and reporting. The area officer in the Leaders Branch would be a less appropriate participant in the exit interview if he assumed other operating duties and did not meet with leaders during the arrival process. The contract agency officer's interest may remain perfunctory even with prodding. One must weigh here the loss to the exit interview of having the interview conducted by a representative of a government agency rather than by the employee of a private institution working under contract with the government. On the other hand, close liaison between a strengthened evaluation staff and a well-staffed reception center, both within the Bureau of Educational and Cultural Affairs, might make interview procedures more effective and the written reports more useful. The leader could still talk with his program officer if he desired, but he would not have to.

One is inclined, on balance, to recommend that the contract agency play the lesser role, that the program officer be invited to participate in any final interview but that he would not necessarily have to attend. It would seem well for the meeting to take place in a reception center office appropriately furnished for a pleasant discussion. At best, the final interview can be an indicator, better for general program analysis than for evaluation of basic changes in an individual's thinking. Adequate information on the interviews should be forwarded to program or area officers by the Department's interviewers along with some over-all evaluation of trends by the evaluation staff.

CONTINUING CONTACTS OVERSEAS

Embassies have been encouraged to maintain relations with returned leaders, and many have done so. The emphasis upon this continuing relationship, using the Leader Program as the bridge, varies greatly. The differences stem in part from the amount of value placed upon the program by the Ambassador, the cultural affairs officer, and other post personnel.

In many areas of the world, an obvious embrace of the returned grantee by American Embassy representatives may be embarrassing to the leader. Where the public welcome home with accompanying public relations fanfare would not noticeably prejudice the position of the leader with his own people, such a welcome is hardly needed. Where such a posture would prejudice the leader's future usefulness, it may negate any possibility of the leader's expressing friendly views or taking helpful action with regard to the United States.

The real problem may be both to prevent overly enthusiastic leaders from saying too much and to find means of maintaining inconspicuous relationships with those who are adversely affected by the visit to America. Continuing relationships should be established by the Embassy on a planned basis—although carried out informally—with all major leaders whether they have been to America under the Foreign Leader Program or not. The precise kind of relationship must depend in part on the climate of opinion in the country, but it must also take into account the personality of individual leaders.

It is a disservice to the United States and to returned leaders when actions by American representatives tend to identify grantees as "our boys" before their own publics. It is better to have a friendly foreign leader judiciously objective than to have him a mere acolyte. With the fundamental goal of the United States defined as assisting portions of the world to achieve political and economic growth toward responsibility and stability, returned leaders must be something more than sycophants worshipping at the American altar. They must be free to think and do what is necessary for the long-range interests of their native lands. This may mean rejection of those parts of the American way, as presently practiced in the United States, that seem inappropriate to present situations in their homelands. This need not offend American sensibilities; the task is to create conditions which in the long run may make possible the evolution of a viable, humane society in each country. Accepting the role of constructive partner among nations as the best means of fulfilling the American mission in the future, what relationship should be maintained with foreign leaders who have returned home?

United States Embassy representatives do chat with returnees at social functions where they may chance to meet. In some instances, cultural affairs officers have called upon returnees some time during the first year after their return, for a friendly visit. In most instances, the leader is offered the opportunity to receive several free subscriptions to American magazines of his choice. When someone active in the Leader Program in the United States and known to many returned leaders happens to be abroad on a specialist grant or a private tour, former leader visitors may be invited to the Embassy or the home of one of the post personnel to meet their friend. Occasionally, former grantees are invited to lecture at American information centers on aspects of American life or on topics related to their specialties.

Evaluative reports are made by the Embassy on the basis of all these contacts, plus whatever public statements may become available, to the Bureau of Educational and Cultural Affairs and are available to the members of the evaluation staff and others in the bureau. Though past bureau leadership has tended to encourage the favorable reports, it has read the full spectrum of comments with interest. Present bureau leadership welcomes more balanced and objective reporting.

Can anything more be done to foster continuing contacts with returned leaders? So much depends upon the specific situation in the country and the personality of the leader that there can be no blanket formula that will suit all cases. Discretion and discrimination, coupled with good taste, are well-worn key words which still have relevance. The Government could do more about stimulating seminars abroad on American life or on problems shared in common with other lands, sponsored by American foundations, drawing in both foreign leaders and American experts. There are also grounds for developing a positive Department attitude toward second visits for an increasing number of foreign leaders. A return trip after five years or a third after ten—if tailored to the needs of the individual selected—may be among the better follow-up devices. In instances when it can be arranged, additional trips under other programs, either private or public, might be even more useful.

The real problem of maintaining better follow-up relations with foreign leaders is related to the broader task of strengthening Embassy relations with many strata of foreign societies. This means knowing the countryside as well as the urban centers. It means more knowledge of local cultures and languages.

7

Departmental Administrative Problems

THE EXCHANGE OF PERSONS program is no longer a neglected stepchild. After functioning under a Deputy Assistant Secretary of State for Public Affairs (for International Information and Cultural Affairs) and later under a Special Assistant to the Secretary of State, the exchange program in the Kennedy administration operates under an Assistant Secretary of State. A Bureau of Educational and Cultural Affairs first emerged in the spring of 1960 with its operational functions (formerly performed by the International Educational Exchange Service) divided between an Office of Educational Exchange and an Office of Cultural Exchange.

A Leaders-Specialists Division existed when the International Exchange Service resided in the custody of the Bureau of Public Affairs. It consisted of three branches: a Foreign Leaders Branch, an American Specialists Branch, and a Foreign Specialists Branch. It took over direction of fourth and fifth branches—the Voluntary Leaders Branch and a Reception Centers Branch—during the temporary existence of the Bureau of International Cultural Relations, and has maintained responsibility for these functions as the Leaders and Specialists Division of the Office of Cultural Exchange in the Bureau of Educational and Cultural Affairs. More recently, the Reception Centers Branch has been eliminated, with direct authority over Department of State reception centers transferred to the chief and assistant chief of the division. At the same time, a seventh reception center was established in Washington, its function presently limited to reception with no programming responsibility.

It was not the purpose of this review of the Foreign Leader Program to make a thorough analysis of the over-all Department of State organization for the conduct of exchange programs. Careful consideration could not be given even to the Leaders and Specialists Division in relationship to the rest of the bureau, for the implementation of recommendations made by the Foreign Service Inspection Corps were still in the initial period when the interviews for this study were conducted. As one officer put it at the time, commenting upon some seven research surveys of exchange programs within a 30-month period, "We are beginning to feel a bit wilted, like the beet the farmer pulled up from the field each day to see how his crop was doing." Some discussion of the bureau's administrative problems is in order only if the restricted view of the bureau gained from primary concentration upon the Leaders Branch is kept in mind and the tentative nature of any suggestions is emphasized.

OPERATIONS: THE DIVISION
AND BRANCH LEVELS

Day-to-day operation of the Foreign Leader Program at the division and branch level is like combating a three-alarm fire. If one part of the program seems safely under control, trouble breaks out elsewhere. The job is frustrating and hectic, demanding men who can handle emergency problems diplomatically, yet with the ability to appraise and improve procedures between crises. The "firefighters" deal with personnel in posts scattered around the globe, other agencies in Washington, other bureaus in the department, or other elements in the Bureau of Educational and Cultural Affairs. They must supervise the contract agencies—not to mention their relations with grantees and contacts with sponsors in local communities across the United States.

The supervisory area officers in the Leaders Branch and their assistant area officers are heavily burdened with detail and have a range of functions which tends to make them Jacks-of-all-trades, with little time to follow through on any of them. About half of their time was consumed until recently in administrative documentation of leader visits, requiring approximately eighteen documents on financial matters and some twenty on programming for each grantee. While the paper flow is somewhat reduced, more of this work could be done by clerical personnel. These officers are responsible for reviewing allocations to and nominations from overseas posts, assigning grantees to contract agencies, giving leaders some orientation concerning their visit to the United States, making certain that all administrative details concerning money and insurance are taken care of, checking with the grantee at the end of a visit in an exit interview, assisting in the orientation of cultural affairs officers assigned to the field, and carrying out a host of other coordinating duties. They no longer greet visitors at the airport, a task assumed by employees of the new Washington reception center.

Their effective authority, however, is not commensurate with their responsibilities. Most of them are young Foreign Service officers, with no previous experience in working with the exchange program. Because of the workload, most of them have not been able to see the Leader Program in action in local communities in the United States. Because of fluctuations in the flow of leaders, there are periods during the year when they have no time for orientation of leaders or cultural affairs officers, for visits to the contract agencies in Washington, for exit interviews with grantees, or for writing reports.

There is a move afoot to put personnel from the Leaders and Specialists Division and the Foreign Leaders Branch in personal contact with program officers in the contract agencies, program sponsors in local communities, and cultural affairs officers overseas. Representatives of the division now participate in a number of conferences in which local community sponsors and representatives of contract agencies participate. Area officers are beginning to be assigned as escorts or interpreters to get first-hand experience with the program in the field. At least three representatives of the division have attended a regional conference of cultural affairs officers overseas. These are recent steps in the right direction. If they were not undertaken earlier, it was in part the result of the stringent staffing pattern which has prevailed throughout the Department. This practice places a premium upon being on the job rather than receiving any form of in-service training. There is growing recognition of the need for further in-service training at the leadership level in both the division and the branch.

If the new Washington reception center were to conduct the arrival and exit interviews with leader visitors, the Leaders Branch would be able to develop further its supervisory, monitoring, liaison, and leadership functions and could assume responsibility for day-to-day operational planning. This latter step would free the bureau's planners to give more attention to long-range planning than has been possible in the past.

PLANNING AND EVALUATION

If the operators are too busy putting out fires to have adequate time for reflection, the planners in the Plans and Development Staff and the evaluators of the Evaluation Branch must be sufficiently withdrawn from program operations to have the time and foresight to look ahead, the objectivity and detachment to survey the present, and an understanding of the past in order to identify broad trends leading to the future. It is too much to expect that the area officers in the Leaders Branch will ever be free to carry out such tasks, although they should be consulted by the planners and evaluators regularly.

Planning and evaluation may be done in relation to the necessities for the next year, the probabilities in the next five years, or the possibilities by the turn of the century. Properly done, such thinking should be done in all three frames of reference, else the short-range necessities crowd out suggestions which might lead to the accomplishment of what may become the long-range imperatives. The need is to develop programs which can meet present problems while looking ahead to future developments. The planning and evaluation functions require broad-gauge personnel of sufficient maturity to be respected by the top leadership of the Bureau of Educational and Cultural Affairs and the Department of State as a whole.

There is necessarily a relationship between these two functions. Evaluation must be able to identify trends and developing problems before they reach catastrophic proportions. To do this requires some knowledge of the changing environment in which a program is functioning—not only what it has been and is now but also what it is likely to become. The criteria of evaluation must be adjusted to these changes and to evolving goals; what might have been good ten years ago and tolerable today may become impossible in five years. On the other hand, planners must look back to know what has been done as a basis for determining where they want to go in the years ahead. Close cooperation between the two functions is essential.

As is the case with almost every part of the Bureau of Educational and Cultural Affairs, the elements performing the planning and evaluation functions are in transition. It is too soon to say definitively whether or not they are moving in the right direction, but some general comment can be made on certain aspects of their current situation. Nothing can reveal the present situation more starkly than the statement of a member of the Plans and Development Staff when asked, "What does the Evaluation Branch contribute to your work?" He replied, "There is no liaison between them and us; no coordination." In part, this unfortunate separation was based on a physical separation of the groups, a situation recently remedied. But there is more to it than that.

The planning function in the past has been quite limited. The regional bureaus of the Department have been exceptionally sensitive to the wishes of the field posts so far as leader exchange planning is concerned. In turn, the Bureau of Educational and Cultural Affairs and its predecessors, with less status, have paid considerable deference to the regional bureaus. As one planner said, "We follow the plan submitted by the post. When Congress appropriates the money, we go down the post priority list until the money runs out." Another put it this way: "Practically everything is determined overseas." A third, who had served as a cultural affairs officer overseas, declared, "We take our lead from the field's requests but we feel the accent has been too heavy on budgeting according to their specifications." Discussing the present function of the Plans and Development Staff, one member said, "We take what the field suggests and coordinate it with suggestions from other sources, balancing it against competing demands of other countries. The staff should be more than a budgeting organization, but the primary tangible result you can see from the staff is budgeting work."

Commenting in a different vein, a staff member expressed the view that "the Plans and Development Staff is here to monitor the program. While it is not directly involved in operations it is watching them to see if anything goes wrong. For example, if an area officer on the staff spots something wrong, he talks to the appropriate officer in the Leaders and Specialists Division, and that officer talks to the program officer in the contract agency in an attempt to correct the situation." This smacks strongly of evaluation or operations rather than planning.

As another indication of why there is not presently a very positive planning role performed by the Plans and Development Staff, an officer in the Leaders Branch said of the planners, "They should keep to long-range matters and not get involved in day-to-day operational planning. After the original plans are set and the funds are allocated, planning should get out of administration. The planning staff is being driven crazy by change sheets." A higher-level leader in the bureau commented, "You can't divorce planning from operations. Each must know the other well, but the planner should not be in on operations. In playing bridge, partners may help plan in the bidding but in the long run one of them plays the hand." It is difficult to disagree with these observations.

The planners should start planning in broader and more long-range terms rather than being so closely concerned with current operations. Their work must, of course, be influenced by budgetary considerations, but they should take a hard and broad look at the future if they are to provide the Department of State and the Congress with farsighted leadership. If the goals of the program are to be realized, grantees must be picked not only as individuals but also as they fit into a broader strategy which the planners should help design. Individual field posts should continue to look at their needs in accordance with their interpretation of the local situation, but there is a responsibility residing in the Plans and Development Staff as well as in the Department of State as a whole to relate these local requests to a broader policy framework.

The evaluation staff, functioning with fewer personnel than the planners and with lower rank, has some able personnel but is not adequately equipped for the successful performance of its function either by numbers, status, breadth of experience, or maturity. The

Department has seemed more interested in hearing favorable comments about the program than in intensive and systematic appraisal, including the identification of emerging problems. Intermittent surveys are not enough. No good driver turns his lights on and off at night, using them only when the road gets bumpy. Evaluation should be an integral and continuing part of the program with a stronger analytical staff than is now available.

STAFFING THE PROGRAM

The conduct of the Foreign Leader Program has been hampered by multiple personnel systems and by the division of responsibilities between the Department of State in Washington and the United States Information Service—the overseas arm of the United States Information Agency. While Foreign Service officers and civil servants may staff the exchange program in Washington, officers of the Information Agency's foreign service are the only exchange staff members who can readily work with the program both at home and abroad.

To gain and maintain an expertise for the conduct of the Foreign Leader Program and other exchange programs, an increasing number of Information Agency foreign service officers have been drawn into exchange posts within the Leaders and Specialists Division and other sections of the Bureau of Educational and Cultural Affairs. This appears to be a desirable development; for the present, these officers should provide the core of the Departmental exchange staff. The services of a number of civil servants are also required in Washington to provide continuity of knowledge and of relationships.

The utilization of Foreign Service officers in staffing exchange programs in Washington can be beneficial to both groups: the Foreign Service officers gain an appreciation of exchange problems, contribute knowledge which they have gained overseas, and help maintain liaison with other parts of the Department of State directed by Foreign Service personnel. In current circumstances, however, it is practically impossible for a Foreign Service officer to pursue a career specialization in the cultural exchange field. So long as the Foreign Service retains its present character and orientation, few will desire to do so. Better foreign service personnel will be provided for the exchange programs if and when the Department gives such programs greater recognition.

Looking beyond the present, there are those who advocate that the United States Information Agency should retain its own personnel system and separate foreign service but be returned to the Department of State in a semi-autonomous position similar to that of the International Cooperation Administration. Along with this change, it is suggested that the exchange programs should be moved from the Department of State to the United States Information Agency and operated by a discrete bureau. This arrangement would reduce problems of dual allegiance and conflicting duties affecting the cultural affairs officers overseas, now more clearly subject to the instructions of their regional directors in the United States Information Agency than to those of the Bureau of Educational and Cultural Affairs in the Department of State. Indeed, it is possible for staff cuts to be imposed upon the United States Information Service in the field at the same time that appropriations are increased for the conduct of the Foreign Leader Program or other exchange programs for which the cultural affairs officers have some responsibility. Although some fear placing exchange programs under the Information Agency, the good sense of future Presidents, Secretaries of State, and directors of the Information Agency could prevent exchange programs from becoming narrow propaganda weapons instead of remaining broad channels of cross-cultural communication.

BUDGET AND FISCAL PROBLEMS

A thorough review of budget and fiscal problems of the Foreign Leader Program would be a study in itself. Like most administrators, those in the Leaders and Specialists Division feel hemmed in financially by bureaucratic restrictions imposed by the Department's own fiscal and legal advisers, by the Bureau of the Budget, by the General Accounting Office, and by the Congress. Because the

Departmental Administrative Problems

Leader Program requires considerable flexibility for the proper handling of its distinguished clientele and is under great pressure to expand the number of leader visitors, it feels these restrictions more acutely than a more routine operation. While some fiscal limitations are a necessity—and often quite useful as a means of helping operators to refuse unwise requests from their clients—there is a need to reduce red tape to a minimum consistent with good administration.

It is a truism that the lower the rank of the administrator the more cautious his interpretation of permissible flexibility. Any battle to gain additional freedom must be waged up through the administrative hierarchy—first within the Department, then in the Bureau of the Budget and the General Accounting Office. These hurdles place demands upon the time and energy of administrators which they can ill afford to divert from daily operations. As a final recourse, the program operator has the option of trying to obtain amendments to the legislative authorization under which his program is conducted. Such an effort is exhausting and perilous because of the possibility that new requirements may be thrust upon the program during the course of reconsideration. Thus the operators tend to exhaust all resources of administrative reinterpretation before venturing into the uncertain legislative arena. Unfortunately, the fiscal relief approved by revised authorizing legislation may never be obtained from the appropriations committees.

Three illustrative problems may suffice to demonstrate the types of budget and fiscal problems confronting the Leaders and Specialists Division. The most serious and immediate problem is the lack of sufficient representation funds. On this issue, the executive branch position is relatively unified; the failure to provide adequate funds can be attributed to the Congress. This is not to say that some individual committees and individual members of the House and Senate are not favorable to providing more adequate allowances to the Bureau of Educational and Cultural Affairs and its contract agencies. Government Accounting Office interpretations have made it clear that under present legislation the Department cannot obtain or spend funds for representation through the contract agencies which it cannot obtain or spend itself.

The appropriations committees, however, have not seen fit to grant more than a pittance to the bureau for representation purposes. The necessity of raising funds from other sources for the entertainment of foreign visitors has taken contract agency time away from programming by forcing the agencies to take on other activities in order to gain the money to entertain leaders. It has meant that in individual communities the Leader Program must rely in large measure on those elements of American society that can pay the entertainment bill, thus tending to limit the leader's exposure to a broader cross section of American life. In some instances, it has meant that ill-paid personnel in centers across America cooperating to conduct the Leader Program have paid costs out of their own pockets to "save" a particular visit, with little hope of recompense.

It is granted that some waste might occur if funds provided for such purposes were increased. But when the present representation allowance of the Bureau of Educational and Cultural Affairs provides approximately ten cents for each visitor to the Leaders and Specialists Division and to the Department's seven reception centers, the danger is not "clear and present." Even such limited funds are not always available for use in emergencies. In one instance a leader was hospitalized while touring America. Because of the serious nature of his condition, his wife and family were brought to the United States on non-Leader Program funds. The leader died before they arrived, but many of their needs were cared for during the course of a brief stay by Department of State reception center personnel. A young staff member spent $25 entertaining these visitors in the period just before their departure but could not be recompensed from the small representation funds his center had available because the visitors were not here on the Leader Program.

A second type of restriction limits the use of an allotment of about $50 per visitor largely to the purchase of books, except in the case of individuals with a special interest in the theater who may use such funds to purchase theater tickets. In view of the limited per diem allowance for leader visitors, which often makes the purchase of theater tickets unfeasible, the Leaders and Specialists Division has sought an interpretation which would allow a leader visitor to spend a portion of the $50 allotment for such a purpose. The broadening of the interpretation was asked on the ground that theater attendance or other forms of cultural activity—as much as materials in written form—help convey to the visitor a full and fair understanding of America. Ten hours of administrative time were expended by the Division upon this matter in a single week with no results. The obstacle this time was in the Department, but it was based upon fear of an adverse ruling by the General Accounting Office.

There is some justification for providing funds which will encourage the visiting leader to take back some materials from America which others can read. Possibly the best solution to the theater ticket problem would be to increase the per diem allowance for each visitor to $25. This could be done without recourse to the Congress. However, such action would increase the program costs per individual and thus decrease the number of visitors within the present budgetary limits. In view of the pressure for an increase in numbers, an adjustment in the per diem is resisted. The increase in per diem would provide a useful solution only if the Leaders and Specialists Division could get a substantial increase in its appropriation. This might entail a move to get a more favorable distribution of funds within the bureau, possibly a struggle on the part of the bureau to compete for more funds within the Department, and probably an attempt by the Department to increase its priority among departments. All of this would only be the prelude to getting such appropriations through the Congress. These facts explain why the program operator, pressed for time though he is, seeks a favorable administrative interpretation to make his program more flexible rather than moving in another direction.

A third illustration also hinges on the problem of the per diem. These payments are advanced twice a month to leaders during the course of their visits. On occasion, because of serious illness in a leader's family or a political crisis at home, a leader must cut his visit short. Even in these emergencies, if the Department does not obtain a refund of the unused per diem funds, the General Accounting Office insists that the Embassy in the leader's country recover these sums. Since the leaders do not always understand the nature of the payments they receive, there are sometimes misunderstandings which diminish the value of the other money expended for the leader's visit. The Department does not have sufficient confidential funds with which to cover such embarrassing situations.

Some have suggested that the legislation should be changed to make such payments in grant form, payable in advance twice a month during their visits. This would make repayment unnecessary. Such a solution would probably be acceptable to the Department of State if it were acceptable to the Congress. Others believe that a change in legislation may not be required but that administrative arrangements might be worked out with the General Accounting Office so that the Assistant Secretary or his deputy in the Bureau of Educational and Cultural Affairs would have the authority to forgive repayments of per diem in appropriate cases. Whether such authority could be negotiated in fact is not known, but in view of the past General Accounting Office position success in this matter is dubious. Whatever solution is to be sought, some action appears necessary in view of the recurring nature of the problem and its negative influence upon the program.

8

Conclusions and Recommendations

THE FOLLOWING SUMMARY highlights the findings of the study by considering the problems, procedures, and accomplishments in the various areas of operation, chapter by chapter. The aim throughout has been to evaluate achievements to date and to suggest improvements in operation that would increase the effectiveness of the program.

1. THE NATURE AND OBJECTIVES OF THE PROGRAM

The Foreign Leader Program of the Department of State annually provides study tours in the United States, averaging forty-five days but sometimes lasting up to sixty or ninety days, for about nine hundred nationals selected for their leadership roles. Evidence gathered by this study suggests that the program has been a significant pioneering experiment in improving relations with these key people and that the effort has been effective in a large majority of cases.

The program has tended, however, to be colored during its developmental stages by the negative motivation of opposing certain regimes and ideologies. It should be more effective if it continues its evolution toward the positive goal of fostering, on a world-wide basis, individual and national security, material well-being, and social progress.

In the past, the purposes of the Foreign Leader Program have been stated so broadly that the personnel involved—both governmental and nongovernmental—have made individual interpretations of the aims that were sufficiently at variance to impede the accomplishment of program objectives.

The Department of State should make clear what values are to govern the programming of typical leaders, as well as those visiting the United States for special purposes, and should make certain that the program implementation in each instance is consistent with the ends chosen.

Typical leaders, here for general purposes, should be free to obtain a full and fair picture of the contemporary American scene so that they may be in a position to present to their own people an accurate and understanding interpretation of the United States and its people. Consultation with colleagues should be only a means toward the accomplishment of this broader goal.

Other objectives may be pursued by leaders who come to the United States to obtain specific knowledge or to fulfill other purposes consistent with, but narrower than, the generally guiding objectives of the program—for example, labor leaders concerned with union problems and educators studying curriculum revision.

2. OVERSEAS AND ARRIVAL PROCEDURES

The types of individuals selected for participation in the program and the orientation they receive will determine in large measure the kinds of substantive experiences and operational procedures that are likely to be most effective in achieving program objectives.

The criteria presently governing selection are generally satisfactory, but they should be applied more rigorously in the case of typical leaders.

The cultural affairs officer of the American Embassy should be recognized as the key figure in the selection process, whatever its formal procedures, under the direction of the American Ambassador and within the "country team." This consideration should be a factor in his appointment, and he should be provided with more adequate staff to make his role effective.

The process of notification should be viewed as part of the orientation procedure and designed to increase the knowledge and the interest of the grantee in the tour. At the same time, information given should be as precise as possible, and expectations concerning the visit should be kept realistic and serious. The wording of the official invitation should stress the study nature of the tour.

Although time for sufficient orientation overseas is likely to be a continuing problem, efforts should be made to impart more objective information about the purposes of the trip and the characteristics of the American scene. The manner of presentation should be adapted to the needs of the individual leader.

The way in which the foreign leader is received at the port of entry is important. The rather routine treatment of the foreign leaders by the inspection services makes it necessary that grantees be received and accompanied through entry procedures by Department of State representatives.

Further negotiations should be conducted in Washington by the Department of State with the departments and agencies responsible for the inspection services regarding means of simplifying entry procedures for leaders, within existing United States laws, and of guaranteeing appropriate Department of State reception center personnel the right to accompany leaders through the entry processes.

Leaders should be received in Washington by experienced employees of the Department of State reception center. The role of the center should be broadened and its staff strengthened so that it may assume responsibility for whatever general departmental orientation is necessary and for introducing the leader to the program officer who will plan the leader's study tour of the United States. This would relieve the Department of State's Leaders Branch of an unnecessary burden.

3. NATION-WIDE PROGRAMMING

The visits of foreign leaders are arranged by three agencies (two nongovernmental, one governmental) which operate under contract with the Department of State and are formally designated as "the contract agencies." They are the Governmental Affairs Institute, the

Committee on Leaders and Specialists of the American Council on Education, and the Office of International Labor Affairs of the Department of Labor. All three agencies are located in Washington, D.C.

With better selection of grantees and more orientation overseas, it would be possible for program officers in the contract agencies to play a more positive role in counseling typical leaders on how to acquire a "full and fair picture of the contemporary American scene."

Presently, under pressure from leader visitors, these officers are scheduling visits to too many communities within a 60-day, or shorter, tour, sending leaders to too many large urban centers, assigning too many to the same cities at the same time, allowing too many professional visits, failing to provide adequate periods of rest and reflection, making inadequate use of pre-trip orientation and terminal centers to provide a framework for interpreting the American scene, designating schedules that involve too many nights in hotels and too few stays in American homes, and failing to discuss frankly the difficulties and frustrations that are likely to occur in such travel.

A few individuals with an exceptional understanding of American life might be allowed greater freedom to arrange their programs outside normal channels. Such procedures should be tested on a limited basis.

Officers in the contract agencies should continue to program most of the foreign leaders. A smaller number of leaders, coming for specific knowledge or special purposes, should be programmed by the Department of State after the establishment of a Special Programs Branch in the Leaders and Specialists Division, provided the necessary funds are placed at the Department's disposal.

Particular attention should be directed toward broadening the experiences of typical labor leaders whose schedules are arranged by the Department of Labor.

Further improvement in programming can be achieved by increased attention to the following areas: (*a*) relations of the contract agencies with the Department of State; (*b*) relations among and within contract agencies; (*c*) in-service training of program officers;

(d) physical facilities of the contract agencies; (e) fluctuation of the workload of program officers; (f) relations of contract agency representatives with overseas posts; (g) biographic information on grantees; (h) knowledge of community resources; (i) relations of contract agencies with local program sponsors; and (j) entertainment and emergency allowances.

The opportunity for one or two pauses for rest and reflection should be available to all visitors but not required. Such opportunities should be arranged so that several leaders might be present at the same time but no formal discussions need be scheduled.

Although the new $20 per diem rate is an improvement over the former $17 rate, it would be desirable to increase the rate further to $25. Individuals brought as specialists but at the leader level should receive the same per diem as regular leader visitors even though the former are programmed through the Foreign Specialists Program.

Some leaders should be programmed in groups, but with greater discrimination as to compatibility of interests and backgrounds. With proper selection of people and itineraries, the group program is a useful device.

4. ORIENTATION AND CROSS-CULTURAL COMMUNICATION

American society can be properly understood by foreign leaders only when seen within a comprehensive perspective which, in most cases, requires intensive pre-trip orientation.

If the program of the Washington International Center can be adapted to their needs, most foreign leaders should be assigned to it for orientation. Something closer to five days for most leaders would be a more fruitful period than the present typical pattern of two days.

Such orientation should continue to be conducted under the direction of a reputable academic organization, but it should be organized on a residential basis. The orientation staff should include a core of permanent personnel plus several outstanding young experts in appropriate fields who would live in residence for one-year periods to conduct seminars and participate in informal discussions. In addition, there is need for distinguished consultants who could be brought in for relatively brief engagements.

These recommendations for intensive pre-trip orientation can be implemented only if there is congressional recognition of this need expressed in adequate appropriations.

The Department of State need for escort-interpreter services has increased 25-fold in the last ten years. It is obvious that the supply to fill such an expanded need has not kept pace with the demand.

The competence of a number of temporary contract escort-interpreters has been criticized by many who have participated in the Leader Program. To help correct this situation, a one-month training program should be established for contract interpreters. Those who show ineptitude in the training course should not be used. Such a program would require the appropriation of additional funds.

Foreign Service officers with language ability, who are in Washington for an interim assignment, should be encouraged to serve as escorts or interpreters to refresh their knowledge of the American scene. Substantial implementation of this recommendation will depend on a much-needed expansion of the Foreign Service.

There are presently shortages of capable escort-interpreters during periods of heavy volume. If the fluctuations could be smoothed out, additional permanent staff could be justified in the Division of Language Services to help meet leader needs.

Over a period of time, individuals who have had experience overseas in the Peace Corps may become a source of competent escort-interpreters.

Outstanding graduate students in American universities and colleges might, on a modest experimental basis, be supported for one or two years of study in a foreign land at government expense with the understanding that they would spend one or two years as escort-interpreters upon their return.

The typical leader—even if he does not need an interpreter of the language—should be offered an escort, who can be an invaluable interpreter of the American culture, but acceptance of an escort should not be obligatory.

5. COMMUNITY PARTICIPATION

The heart of the Foreign Leader Program is the personal contacts and experiences arranged by local program sponsors in communities across the country. Participants in community programming are to be praised for their extraordinary expenditure of time, energy, and money. In spite of a growing awareness of the shortcomings of local programming, many problems remain, a number caused by lack of sufficient financial support.

These local programming problems include the following: (*a*) Too many discussions are scheduled with counterparts of the leaders; (*b*) Schedules include excessive concentration on viewing physical facilities; (*c*) Area study institutes on university campuses are overused; (*d*) Insufficient attention is devoted in most cities to the exploration and cultivation of new resources; (*e*) Too many leaders arrive overtired so that only the most tentative scheduling can be arranged ahead of time; (*f*) Visits to industries and businesses tend to be underemphasized with too few resources from which leaders can choose; (*g*) Visiting labor leaders are restricted too much to a labor-oriented program almost to the exclusion of a broader view; (*h*) Few leaders have sufficient opportunity to pursue chance contacts established outside the formal program; (*i*) The typical leader spends too much time in public accommodations, missing opportunities for family experiences of greater import to the basic purposes of the program; (*j*) Local sponsors are subjected to fluctuating workloads which make programming difficult; and (*k*) Some of the physical facilities of local sponsors are unsuitable in efficiency and appearance.

Salaries paid to personnel employed by local sponsors are too low to attract and hold able personnel for long-term careers.

The intermittent availability of most volunteer workers contributes to administrative inefficiency.

No type of local sponsor appears to have sufficient funds, or can foresee such funds from available resources in the near future, to provide adequate staff and facilities.

A strong case can be made for the establishment of five additional

Department of State centers to provide regional leadership and supervision for the Leaders and Specialists Division. For the present and as a possible transition phase, it is recommended that small regional field offices, without programming functions, be established at strategic locations to provide regional supervision and guidance. Staffs of existing reception centers[1] should be strengthened to assume field office responsibilities.

More generous agreements should be negotiated with sponsors in heavily used cities to cover all expenses of programming and reporting. In less-used cities, contracts might provide for basic administrative costs essential to the provision of central leadership and stable staffing. In even more marginal cities, where programming cannot be a full-time job, some formula of assistance based on payment of basic administrative costs for each visitor might be worked out. These steps will require substantial appropriations.

Even in operations under local contracts, private initiative can be stimulated through the use of advisory committees and the local raising of funds for special projects. It may be that more funds can be raised for special causes which appear useful to local people than for general administration.

As local sponsors build professional staffs and their governing boards become more representative of the broad range of organized groups, labor union sponsors should be encouraged to transfer much, or all, of the programming of labor visitors to the local sponsors handling other leaders.

The role of local program officers and experienced private individuals in assisting foreign leaders to interpret their experiences before they move on to other communities needs to be strengthened. More time for this should become available if leaders visit fewer communities and remain for longer periods.

6. TERMINAL PROCEDURES

The importance of a terminal seminar just before the leader departs for home has not been sufficiently recognized. This should be

---

[1] The seven Department of State reception centers are at New York, New Orleans, San Francisco, Seattle, Miami, Honolulu, and Washington.

a carefully planned part of every tour, and should be followed up by a representative of the American Embassy after the leader returns home.

Attendance at three-day residential terminal seminars, under staff and auspices similar to the recommended pre-trip orientation program, should be a requirement for all typical leader visits under this program.

In current circumstances, few leaders are in a position to make a balanced assessment of either program procedures or substantive observations as they race through exit interviews. The escort-interpreters have been more valuable than exit interviews in assessing the departing leaders' program experiences.

The number of exit interviews for each visitor should be reduced to one and that should be conducted by the new Department of State reception center in Washington, properly staffed for this purpose. The interview with the program officer in the contract agency would become optional.

The present variety of continuing contacts with leaders overseas provides many opportunities both for evaluating program results and for maintaining relations established by the program. More could be done to stimulate private foundations to schedule seminars abroad, involving both foreign leaders and American experts, on American life and problems shared with other nations.

Although second visits are possible under the Foreign Leader Program, the current passive attitude toward such visits should be reconsidered. Depending upon the climate of opinion in a participant's country, additional visits under this or other programs could be a most effective kind of follow-up.

The improvement of relations with returned leaders is dependent to some extent upon the general strengthening of Embassy contacts with people at all levels in other societies.

The United States Government should expect leaders, once they have returned to their homelands, to think and act according to what they believe is necessary for the long-range interests of their own lands. It should not be offended if they publicly reject those elements of "the American way" that they believe are inappropriate to present conditions in their countries. The task is to help them create conditions which in the long run make possible the evolution of viable, humane societies, consistent with both their own traditions and those of the United States.

7. DEPARTMENTAL ADMINISTRATIVE PROBLEMS

The reorganization in the spring of 1960 of the Department of State bureau responsible for the conduct of the Foreign Leader Program is just beginning to have effect. Thus suggestions concerning the new Bureau of Educational and Cultural Affairs must necessarily be tentative.

Area officers in the Leaders Branch remain heavily burdened with administrative detail, some of which might be eliminated or delegated to clerical personnel. Their present participation in the arrival and exit processes might well be made the responsibility of the new Washington reception center. Their functions should be primarily supervisory but should include responsibility for short-range operational planning.

The Plans and Development Staff should be freed from operations and should assume a more active role of leadership and program planning.

More effective use could be made of the Evaluation Branch if its staff were strengthened and its function given greater emphasis.

For the present, the core of the Departmental exchange staff should be drawn from among foreign service officers of the United States Information Agency, supplemented by civil servants and regular Foreign Service officers.

A brief review of the Leader Program's budget and fiscal problems points to the fact that because of budget limitations much administrative time is expended in trying to attain a degree of flexibility in the use of the funds available so that program goals may be achieved.

These limitations on the use of funds—often a serious block to program implementation—might be somewhat reduced by further negotiation within the Department and with the General Accounting Office. In some instances, new legislation would have to be sought.

The recommendations made above suggest that the program

should be assigned a higher priority and larger budget by the Department, the Bureau of the Budget, the President, and the Congress.

An especially pressing need of the Foreign Leader Program is an increase in representation and emergency funds and more flexible provisions for their use.

It is recommended that the name of the program be changed and that it be known as the "Leader Program" of the Department of State, with visitors categorized as coming under the "Leader Program (General)" or the "Leader Program (Special)," the former to be programmed by the contract agencies and the latter by a new Special Programs Branch of the Leaders and Specialists Division.

Appendixes

APPENDIX A.—NUMBER OF COMPLETED LEADER Visits,*
FISCAL YEARS 1956–1960

Country of Origin	1956	1957	1958	1959	1960	1961	Total Persons
Latin America	135	254	213	187	211	212	1,000
Europe	375	356	274	240	201	403	1,446
Far East	123	219	160	215	149	146	866
Near East & South Asia	104	102	92	117	90	146	505
Africa	21	28	42	46	63	165	200
Total	758	959	781	805	714	926	4,017

* These figures exclude so-called voluntary leader visitors who were programmed by the Department of State but bore their own costs. The increase in number of visitors in fiscal year 1957 was made possible in part by the limitation of most grants since the start of that fiscal year to 60 instead of 90 days. *Source:* Bureau of Educational and Cultural Affairs, Department of State.

APPENDIX B.—PROGRAM COSTS OF LEADER EXCHANGES*: OBLIGATIONS, FISCAL YEARS 1956–1960

Area	1956	1957	1958	1959	1960	Total Grant Costs
Latin America	$219,773	$588,784	$593,623	$732,583	$820,016	$2,954,779
Western Europe	612,762	1,093,763	660,824	692,815	724,687	3,700,851
Eastern Europe	—	—	90,722	57,014	138,639	286,475
Far East	367,242	826,197	928,815	765,866	513,053	3,401,173
Near East & South Asia	453,010	500,612	563,903	559,636	627,370	2,714,531
Africa	(a)	134,592	276,933	248,121	405,670	1,065,316
Total	$1,652,787	$3,143,948	$3,114,820	$3,056,035	$3,229,435	$14,197,025

* These figures do not include the cost of domestic and overseas staff. The increase in grant costs in fiscal year 1957 resulted in part from larger per diem payments to individual grantees and a larger payment per grantee to the contract agencies. *Source:* Bureau of Educational and Cultural Affairs, Department of State.

(a) Combined with Near East and South Asia.

APPENDIX C.—BUREAU OF EDUCATIONAL AND CULTURAL AFFAIRS, DEPARTMENT OF STATE

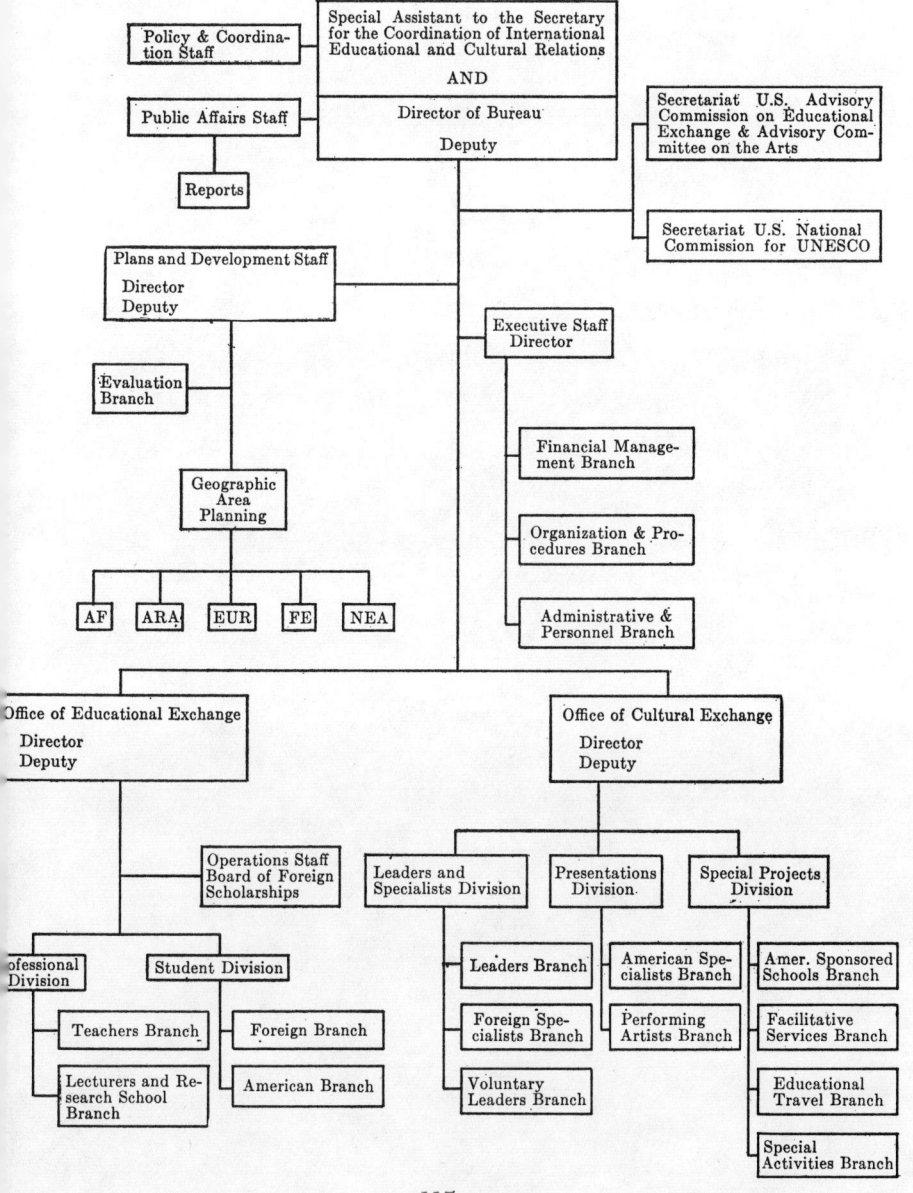

- Special Assistant to the Secretary for the Coordination of International Educational and Cultural Relations AND Director of Bureau / Deputy
  - Policy & Coordination Staff
  - Public Affairs Staff
    - Reports
  - Secretariat U.S. Advisory Commission on Educational Exchange & Advisory Committee on the Arts
  - Secretariat U.S. National Commission for UNESCO
  - Plans and Development Staff — Director / Deputy
    - Evaluation Branch
    - Geographic Area Planning
      - AF
      - ARA
      - EUR
      - FE
      - NEA
  - Executive Staff — Director
    - Financial Management Branch
    - Organization & Procedures Branch
    - Administrative & Personnel Branch
  - Office of Educational Exchange — Director / Deputy
    - Operations Staff Board of Foreign Scholarships
    - Professional Division
      - Teachers Branch
      - Lecturers and Research School Branch
    - Student Division
      - Foreign Branch
      - American Branch
  - Office of Cultural Exchange — Director / Deputy
    - Leaders and Specialists Division
      - Leaders Branch
      - Foreign Specialists Branch
      - Voluntary Leaders Branch
    - Presentations Division
      - American Specialists Branch
      - Performing Artists Branch
    - Special Projects Division
      - Amer. Sponsored Schools Branch
      - Facilitative Services Branch
      - Educational Travel Branch
      - Special Activities Branch